SAINT FRANCIS OF ASSISI

Also by Marisa Calvi with Kuthumi Lal Singh
"You Don't Have Problems, You're Just Bored!"
"Pharaoh Thutmose III (Let's Go For A Walk; Book One)"
"Pythagoras of Samos (Let's Go For A Walk; Book Two)"
"Balthasar the Magus (Let's Go For A Walk; Book Three)"

available via www.newenergywriting.com

SAINT FRANCIS OF ASSISI

A LIFE ADVENTURE OF ASCENDED MASTER KUTHUMI AS TOLD TO MARISA CALVI

First published in 2015 by
Marisa Calvi
20 Pinus Avenue
Glenorie NSW 2157
AUSTRALIA

A CIP catalogue record for this book is available
from the National Library of Australia

ISBN; 978-0-9803506-7-8 (paperback)
978-0-9803506-8-5 (e-book)

Cover artwork;
Detail from "Saint Francis in Prayer" by Caravaggio (1606)

for my soul

KUTHUMI'S INTRODUCTION

My life as Saint Francis of Assisi was not an exclusive experience. Many have allowed their souls into his life to contribute to the legacy that he left for humanity. This is true for many beings who have had a profound effect upon consciousness; Yeshua being another one.

Here is where things can get tricky. You see I now write to you from my sovereign energy, from the state of pure ascension, where I am completely integrated. I do not have the weight of beliefs or the gravity of the human existence to shape how I perceive reality.

I am beyond the limits of time and space and I rejoice in that freedom. The linearity of being human is the biggest deterrent for me in choosing to live another human lifetime. Linearity can be so tedious.

I can sit in my circle of completion, with the limitless connection of my soul and watch all that you are doing upon your Earth. I see you choose lifetime after lifetime. I also see you jumping back and forth within your timeframes; one life in Ancient Egypt, then one in Medieval times, then way back to Mesopotamia, then forward to a time that has not even been known.

You think you are living out lifetimes in a linear way, but this is far from what you do. You are a soul having experiences and that will never be limited by time or space.

You relive lifetimes for the joy of diving back in, to know it another way. You open awareness in one and it sends ripples of energy back through all you have known, to expand your connection with all you have allowed yourself to know of living.

And thus you can share experiences of a lifetime with others, and this is what I did with Saint Francis. The story I will share with you is my story of Saint Francis. It is my experience of this incredible life. I sit within my ascended state and I recall my experience of one version of this lifetime.

So now once again, as you sit in your experience, I invite you to take my hand and visit another of mine.

When you are ready, let's go for walk....

CHAPTER ONE

I would so love to skip over the details of my childhood which seem so trivial and inconsequential when compared to what I did within my adult years. However upon reflection I can see how these years shaped me.

We create beginnings to set upon a path. However the path has twists, turns, detours and even road blocks. It is how we choose to deal with these moments on the journey that shape our character and who we become. So I will share with you those moments which helped form me.

The family I was born into were wealthy beyond the means needed for living a comfortable life. We were not rich in warmth and affection though, but to my parents they provided what they felt life required. I learnt from a very early age that their loving attention was not something available to me and so I found my comfort in my surrounds and my belongings.

I had those who were paid to care for me but they too knew that our home was not that for frivolity and overt kindness. One of my earliest memories is of a maid playing peek-a-boo with me. Each time she pulled her hands from her face and cried "Boo!" I would squeal with delight.

Soon my father appeared, looming over her like a shadow.

"Are you trying to make him weak?" he said through a tightly held jaw.

"No, Sir," she answered quietly.

"Then stop that immediately," he spat.

I can still remember how red her face was and how she would not even glance at me as she turned to walk away.

The next day I ran to find her. She acted as though she could not see me and I pulled at her skirt.

"Not today, young Sir," she said without even looking at me and made way to do some other chore.

I felt it then so strongly. I was barely three years but I could feel it; that there could be no joy in this home. There was no place for it. Even if it did find its way here, my father would crush it in any way that he could.

Each year as I grew I understood this more and more. I saw the servants steal smiles between each other when my parents were not around. I heard them talk with humour once behind closed doors and away from the charade that they acted out in the presence of the family.

So too I found my own way to have my joy. To create a sacred space so I could still allow it into my life.

My toys would come alive when I was alone. A wooden horse would whinny and snort, then run across the room. A doll would smile and tell me how much he liked me. A stuffed bear would push his face into mine and giggle. They were small moments but they kept something within my heart alive so that when I had to be with my parents there was the knowing that I would soon have respite from their austere countenance.

I was walking with one of the servants one day, my hand sitting within her stiff hand, her eyes looking ahead in a blank stare. Now at five years old I knew not to make conversation as even far from the house she would still be too scared to say or do anything that I may repeat, intentionally or otherwise.

We had been sent from the house for "air and exercise to ensure my vigour" at my father's request. I also believe he may have caught me talking to my toys and was scared I was indeed becoming "soft". So each afternoon a servant would come and gather me, bundle me in a coat and drag me out to walk.

On this particular afternoon a very young girl was sent out with me for the first time. She was barely fifteen and I could tell as she readied me for the walk she was far from comfortable about being responsible for me.

"Just don't lose him!" the head maid had laughed as she assigned her to me for the day.

We stepped out of the house and I could see her looking around, unsure of which way to head.

"We go there," I said pointing to the left and completely lying. We never went that way so I decided to try my luck with this first timer and within seconds that was the direction that we walked.

There was a reason I was never walked that way as it led out of the privileged area I lived in. Soon the grand houses fell away to be replaced by shacks and shanties. Some were even built against the other to hold one another up.

To the maid with me it was not so much of a shock as this is where she lived. It didn't even occur to her that I should not be there, which was perfect. To me this place was full of wonder. I could smell food cooking that seemed pungent and distasteful. I saw children my age run through the streets screaming and hollering. Then I even heard an adult shouting a profanity and the maid looked down at me.

"Do not ever say that word! Do you hear me?" she snapped.

I nodded my head and smiled, storing the word away for later use.

"I should not have walked you this way. I cannot believe the others do," she muttered and turned us around to walk back home.

As she did I saw a young woman come out of a doorway. She was not much older than the maid with me. A young child ran towards her and as he got closer she bent down so she could scoop the boy up in her arms, pulling him close and then nuzzling his neck, making him laugh.

"Oh he is playing with his maid too," I said.

"Maid? Oh you silly boy, there are no maids here. That is his mother," she sighed.

I turned to look at them again. Now the woman had swung the child so he sat upon her hip and was bouncing him while she sang.

I did not see any poverty here. I did not see houses about to fall apart or the clothes that were threadbare. All I saw was a mother and child sharing love and affection and something within me asked why joy seemed to be here and yet not in my home.

As we walked back into the upper class district, I saw the houses get bigger and more solid. I saw the clothes grow thicker, tighter and darker. Faces were clean and hair was short or swept into pinned rolls, or hidden beneath hats or scarves. Everything was once more constrained and restrained.

Fences and gateways closed off each home and we walked into the area claimed by my father's money. There were no sounds to be heard and the only smells were that of the oils the servants used to ensure the home held the fragrance of roses and lilies.

My coat was taken from me.

"Now go play with your toys," the maid said simply and nodded to my playroom.

I sat once more amongst my toys and held a small wooden figurine whose arms and legs were moveable. I took the arms and arranged them just as the young mother had; forward and ready to catch her son. I tried to imagine my mother's face upon the toy but it would not appear.

"Maybe I could ask her for a hug," I thought and went to find her in the parlour where she would be doing some needlework.

"What is it Francisco?" she said looking over the frame of her embroidery.

I walked towards her and put my arms around her waist, then rested my head upon her lap. I heard her take a deep sigh, then she gently stroked my head.

This lasted only a minute before she said softly, "It's time to ready for dinner. Go and wash."

I lifted my head and offered her a smile but she hid her face behind her sewing once more. The moment had been enough though. I went to find a maid to help me wash.

I was lucky enough to have siblings and therefore some company but in honesty I never truly felt connected to any of them. My sisters bonded with their feminine interests and my brothers formed into the reserved proper males that my father wished them to become. There was a familiarity but no deep resonance. There was not even camaraderie to plot mischief the way that children do. We had been trained and disciplined too well to even think of such things. The retribution we would face would be too harsh to even risk.

I did not think it so unusual at the time as I knew of no other way to be within a family. I also now see it as a blessing. Family ties can be the hardest to let go of when one decides to pursue their own path, and my parents by way of their detachment provided me with a valuable gift to eventually know myself without that burden.

However I was still human and a youthful one at that. I craved some connection and knowing that it would not come from within my family I sought it elsewhere.

My schooling provided it to me by way of my schoolmates. Here there were other young men of my age and background. We were all wealthy and without any of the concerns that most people had to live by. In fact the only purpose of our education was to entertain us and make use of our time until we could follow our fathers into their businesses.

We learnt to read and know numbers so we could manage and maintain our wealth and possessions. We studied so we could read of far off places and then travel there with knowledge. Our education was to make us acceptable to the class we were born into. It was a system to maintain the bubble of society we had been birthed within.

I found school incredibly easy. To say I was intelligent was an understatement. My mind could grasp knowledge like a predator and devour it. I was well read and this made me very appealing to seek for conversation, so I made friends easily.

I soon became part of a group of young, wealthy men with no concerns apart from our studies. We had no need to rush home to partake of chores. There were no fields to tend to or homes to mend. Such things were taken care of by our parents' wealth. Instead we could while away our time in taverns and bars, ordering wine and food with no care for the price.

This socialising became my sanctuary. I did not indulge so in the wines as others did. I did not care for how it clouded my thinking, let alone my ability to walk. Besides, my father who allowed my extracurricular activities to gain standing with other families would never have tolerated such behaviour nor to return to his home in such a state. I revelled in the conversations. I philosophised about politics and history. I shared what I imagined Africa or Britannia would be like. I also listened to what others shared of their home lives and within this I learnt my life was not so different.

"I remember the last time my mother learnt she was pregnant," slurred Marco one night. "She cried for days. I heard her ask my father if the doctor might give her something to get rid of it."

"I cannot remember the last time my father spoke of anything but his business with me," Luca told me one night.

I looked at the six of us, all born into privilege but with little to no affection and I wondered what fathers we would become. I felt something inside me say "Don't become one" and in that moment I truly shuddered at the thought of not having my own family.

How could I marry and not have children? Well there were many marriages that were without children but that was not something I believed one could control.

Then something just as instantly washed through me and I felt the freedom to not marry and not have children. I did not have to choose that path and it was quite easy for a man to do this in my time. Sure, it may not seem the normal choice but it would be acceptable. I could just avoid any courtship and make another life.

I thought of sharing this with my friends but I knew several were already betrothed or had been made to court young women approved by their family. My parents were still setting out such plans for my older siblings and had not thought of me yet. So I said nothing.

Some people are happy to keep upon the course laid out for them. It saves a lot of anguish and thinking. To me it was the opposite. The more I thought about staying on the path set for me by my parents, the more turmoil it brought up within me. In my teenage years I had the innate feeling that my life would not turn out how it was expected to. I just had no idea how it actually would.

CHAPTER TWO

The years between child and man were when I felt my mind truly begin to change. I always had a wonderful relationship with my mind. I saw it as like a torch within the dark. It showed me truth and clarity as a child. Now as I grew older and gained some more independence I felt it begin to open up in a way which delighted me.

As a child my mind was like a catapult. Its constant scouring for knowledge pushed me to look at my surrounds with a thoroughness which I believe helped me see much that others would miss. I do not just mean in actual objects around me, but that I felt I saw much more than what the eye could simply take in. I would walk through the marketplace or town square, my mind encouraging me to take in everyone and everything that I passed. Then it would invite me to do more; my mind would let me see more.

I could watch some men talking and though they did not appear to argue I could sense hostility. I could see a young girl scurry past me and knew she was in a hurry for her chamber pot at home. I am certain now that many times it was merely fantasy and storytelling that I made to entertain myself, but I do not care. For I know deep in my being, it was actually my heart teaching me to open my senses.

Around the age of fifteen is when I truly felt this shift. It sometimes made it hard to be around others especially when they did not seem to be as open as I was.

"You can be a real sour apple to be around sometimes," Luca spat at me one night in the tavern.

"I haven't said anything tonight!" I protested.

"Exactly! You sit there as though we are of no interest for you to interact with," he proclaimed.

Unfortunately it was true. Some nights their conversation and banter were truly tedious. I soon learnt those were the nights to drink some more but still in moderation. This provided excuse for any lack of conversation. It also made it easier to keep a smile upon my face and not seem so dreary.

Those were also the nights when sleep would be so deep that my dreams could be frightening enough to remind me of why I had chosen restraint with alcohol. It would also be the nights my brother Pietro, with whom I shared a room, would wake me by twisting my nose with such force it could bleed as punishment for waking him with my drunken snores.

So I sought more ways to spend time with myself. I would head to the outskirts of Assisi and find a quiet spot upon the mountainside. Once there my mind was free of distractions and it could have me all to itself. In solitude and stillness it could barrage me with questions or ideas so that minutes could feel like hours.

Then on other days there would be nothing but silence. At first these periods scared me as I thought perhaps I was losing my intelligence which I adored. I would push my mind asking what was happening.

In response I would get one word: "listen".

Listen to what? If there was no internal dialogue then what was there to listen to? Well there were the birds, the breeze in the trees and the distant sound of a horse cart but not much else. I listened anyway, closing my eyes to focus even more and soon I was hearing what was in-between the sounds. There is much to hear in silence and words cannot explain it. I highly recommend everyone tries it sometime as I know it was what allowed that beautiful shift to begin to open within me.

It took many times though before I truly felt the beauty of this. To stop and let my thoughts subside as though there simply was nothing to think about. I had heard that the Buddhists in the east used such methods but that had always seemed like some exotic ritual that was necessary for their mystical religion.

My Catholicism had shown me the power of prayer and that was taught to me as a dialogue with God. Well not really even a dialogue. It was more like a request or application. You weren't expected to hear anything in return. That honour was held for the prophets and saints, and I as a silk merchant's son was hardly in either category.

I sat within our church one day as our local bishop served mass. He called upon us to pray for our salvation from the original sin which had damned us to the rigours of human life. I dropped my head and repeated the words of the prayer we had been taught, as everyone else's recitations blurred around me. The words stopped from my mouth soon after they began and I lifted my head. I looked to the images of Christ upon the walls around me. Above the altar was the scene of the crucifixion and I wondered what was in Christ's mind as he slowly had his human life taken from him.

My eyes followed down his body, from the blood upon his brow drawn by the thorns of his crown, past his punctured wrists, the slash upon his side and then the single nail forcing his feet together. It was as I looked at the blood at his feet that I realised the bishop was looking at me, and though his mouth was still leading the congregation in the words of the prayer he may as well have been yelling, "What are you doing?"

I pulled my head back down and finished the prayer with the others.

I was not embarrassed at what I had done, or at being "caught" by the bishop. I knew within that act of breaking away from the congregation, in pulling myself from the mindless parroting of a prayer, I had allowed myself a perfect moment with Christ. In allowing myself my own reflection upon his image, I had stopped the unconscious relationship I had with him. I connected with his truth and I did it more powerfully than any prayer could have guided me.

It was a perfect moment of truth for me and how I would come to know God.

In that time of simply looking upon his image with a clear mind, seeing between the paint strokes, listening between the words of the prayer, I opened up a new connection with spirit that would guide me for the rest of my life.

CHAPTER THREE

I had always enjoyed attending church for whatever reason, whether it be the Sunday service from a sense of duty or for celebrations such as a marriage or a baptism. As a child the church was to me like a haven and a true sanctuary from the monotony of everyday life. In its walls I could escape into a world of myths and legends which were both supernatural and at the same time helped me see the design of our human life.

As I approached manhood though my mind, in its passion to have me see everything as intricately as possible, started with questions that my child mind would never have pondered. I looked upon the priests and their hierarchy and wondered if Jesus would have approved of this. I wondered how pure these men's hearts were. As much as I would have loved to truly believe that their commitment to serve God would make them thus, a part of me was not so certain.

Soon I was sitting within the church and looking upon them as they prayed, preached and poured their communion wine, trying to see if I could measure their connection to their actions. I saw weariness in the older one's eyes. I could sense a fire in a new acolyte. I also felt frustrations in the ones who seemed to be regretting their vows.

One day at mass, I noticed one of the older men was missing from the altar. It was Father Antonioni, who had served there for over twenty years.

"He must be ill," I whispered to my sister beside me.

Elisabetta giggled as she put her gloved hand in front of her mouth. "Oh Francisco! You did not hear? He was found in the bed of Luisa Pancioni. Her husband found them. Father Antonioni is now in a monastery far from here."

I slumped back in the pew, utterly astounded. I had not enjoyed the questions that my mind had made me ask of these men. I had avoided even feeling into the truth of what it wanted to show me. However now I knew: no man is secure against sin no matter his connection or devotion to God.

There was no path that could make you immune. I looked around me at all those sitting in the church. What sins did they commit each day? Were they here because it would absolve them or were they here to give them the strength to resist the temptations when they would next present themselves?

It was too much to even think about or comprehend. I took a deep breath, resisting the urge to release it as a sigh. Instead as I slowly breathed out I once more looked up at Jesus upon his cross above the altar. He had died to save us from sin and yet twelve hundred years later we seemed to have not truly learned or appreciated his sacrifice for us. We were not cleansed. We were no better than those he had walked amongst.

As I looked upon him now, I saw the expression of pain upon his face as being more anguished than ever before. He did not look to the heavens in turmoil to question his fate or his circumstance. Jesus looked to God to pray that one day we could truly accept and embrace what he had done for us. His pain was in knowing that his one act would never truly cleanse us. All it could ever be was to serve as a reminder of the pure life we could choose in his name.

I wished I could change that carving every time I went to church after that. I would not have had Jesus looking to his father. Instead I would have him looking down at all of us so when you looked upon him, he looked upon you. In his eyes he would ask the question of all us:

"Do you choose a life without sin?"

It would not be to instil fear or to make us feel impure, but as an inspiration to live a life with joy for the gift of being part of God's creation.

CHAPTER FOUR

Much can be said of our challenges in life and how they provide us with lessons. Within the wealth of my family life, it would seem that such problems would be far and few and they were. Even the emotional distance my parents kept from me was not such a hardship when compared to how some lived.

So to some I seemed sheltered in my younger years and I agree that I was. I did not know hardship in the way so many did. I see now that the comforts provided by my family made the few trials I faced even more significant and provided me with dramatic opportunities to grow. The most telling of these is one that is still retold today as a key to what would lie ahead. To me personally it was also a greater connection to the teachings and wisdom of Christ.

As part of my duties to my father in learning his business I would often be the one chosen to attend the local market to trade on his behalf. Sometimes this would be when he was travelling to source new goods, or that he would simply push me to the door on a day he felt poorly.

"It is time you took more responsibility and learned the ways of doing business," he would explain.

Outside I would be met by a servant who had loaded bolts of cloth upon a cart. He would nod simply and then begin to push it to the markets while I walked silently by his side. I will admit I enjoyed trade; the banter with the customers, being able to show my knowledge of the cloths I was selling and of course taking the time to feel between the words spoken by us both.

It was on a day that was warm and trade was brisk. I saw the man making his way through the markets. He was dressed in rags that scarcely covered him. His feet were bare and his beard was rough and shaggy. He stopped at each trader holding out his hands with hardly time to ask for alms before they waved him away. I watched in horror as one man even pushed him.

When he came to me I reacted as I had been trained to do so and as we all had.

"I have nothing for you," I said plainly and turned away.

He shuffled on and I turned back to watch him leave the marketplace empty-handed.

Something inside me burned as I watched him make his way. The voice that had come out of me hadn't even felt like it was mine. In it I heard my father or any one of the other traders or wealthy men who had more than enough to spare such a man.

I looked at the bolts of cloth before me and they now looked different. I no longer saw exquisite weaving and immaculate embroidery. Now I just saw opulence and extravagance. No one needed such fabric to wear or decorate their homes. A plain material could do the same thing.

I closed my eyes and saw Christ upon his cross, draped in the simplest of loincloths and then the burn in my heart almost made my chest explode. In refusing the beggar I had refused him the most basic of Christ's lessons; that of honour and compassion for our fellow man. Every merchant in the marketplace had also neglected this and yet each one of us would make way to church and sit there saying our prayers as though we were holy and just.

My stomach turned the more I thought about it.

"Can you believe it?" a trader beside me muttered. "Assisi used to be so noble and—and—clean! Now we have to have such low living beings walk our streets."

I turned to him with a look of disbelief.

"Would our Lord and Saviour have been so dismissive of him?" I asked, genuinely curious as to what he would answer.

He laughed out loud at this. "Our Lord and Saviour would ask this man why he had not worked harder to provide for himself," he finished and laughed again.

I bit my lip to fight against responding to him and made as though to tidy the silks and velvets upon my cart.

Thankfully soon the day's trade was over. My servant appeared and lifted the handles on the cart so as for us to begin our way home.

"You go ahead. I have one last meeting to attend to," I said. Then I set off in the direction the beggar had walked.

I was soon within another square of Assisi. There was a fountain in the centre that also served as a well for homes nearby. The beggar was sitting on the edge of the fountain chewing on some bread he had been gifted. I smiled when I saw him, glad he had found some food, but then the way he was eating it made the heat within me rise up again.

It seemed like each mouthful was to save his life. There was no pleasure in this eating, no savouring of flavour or indulgence of a craving. This was simply survival for him; a morsel so he could exist for another day.

I walked up to his side and as he saw my shadow upon the ground he stopped eating and looked up.

"I will move on Sir. I just needed a moment to eat and drink before I make my way," his voice shook as he spoke.

"There is no need for you to leave. Have all the time you need," I said and with that I handed him my purse with all the earnings of the day, as well as my personal money. "Take this and truly feed yourself. Buy some clothes and even a room for some time."

He did not move for a while, just looked upon the purse. I wondered if he thought it was some test or a joke. When he gazed into my eyes though he knew it was neither. His hand came forward and took the purse. The weight alone was enough to let him know it was a significant amount.

"People will think I have stolen this," he said and I saw even more fear and despair grow in his eyes.

I shook my head. "No, they will not. Tell them you prayed and it was gifted to you by Francisco di Bernardone. I will vouch for your honesty."

When I arrived home my father was waiting for me in the parlour and called out to me.

"Come show me how successful your day was. I saw what was missing from the cart. You did well, now I would like to see just how well. Hand me the purse," he said.

I took a deep breath and I am sure my face turned red.

"I do not have the purse," I said barely above a whisper.

"What did you say? Speak up when you answer me," he said leaning forward in his chair.

"I do not have the purse," I repeated slightly louder. I knew there was unpleasantness to come and found some resolve to face it.

My father stood now and approached me. "Were you robbed?" he asked and for a moment I could actually feel there was some concern for me. Then it was gone. "I see no marks upon you of a struggle, nor are your clothes torn. So what happened to my money?"

"I gave it to someone in need," I said and closed my eyes.

"A beggar?"

I nodded and kept my eyes closed.

"All of it?"

I nodded once more.

"Have you any idea of how much money there was?"

My head lifted and dropped again. Then I spoke once more.

"We did not need it. He did. He was days from death if he did not have money for food and shelter. It was God's will that I did this. Christ himself told me to do this in honour of all that he taught."

My eyes were still closed when his fist hit me the first time. Within that one blow I felt all that my father wished to convey about my actions and my explanation. I swayed upon my feet and opened my eyes. When I saw my father lifting his arm again ready to bring it down upon me I knew this was far worse than I could have anticipated.

His curled hand was joined by the other to strike me over and over. I wrapped my arms around my head and fell to my knees but he would not stop and I knew no amount of pleading would steady his rage. Instead I surrendered.

In that moment of surrender I found some peace to escape the pain. I imagined Christ being struck and whipped upon his arrest. I saw him pushed to the ground as he carried his cross. I escaped into his story to save myself.

My father though felt this and pulled at one of my arms to reveal my face. He leant down as close as he could and I felt his spit as he spoke.

"So weak! You do not even fight back as you know you are wrong!"

I knew I was far from wrong.

The next day the soreness served not as continuing punishment from my father as he had hoped. Instead each time I felt an ache or saw one of the many bruises I remembered the good I had done. Each moment of pain was pure and worthy and I relished every moment of what some would call suffering.

My father openly sneered when he saw me now. At the dinner table he would scowl at me, hoping to make eye contact so he could directly insult me again but I would not indulge his anger anymore.

"Pietro, you will attend the market from now," he announced in front of my entire family. "I can trust you."

This made me want to laugh out loud. In his endorsement of Pietro he had hoped to humiliate me but instead all I felt was freedom. There would be no more manipulation of another to extract their money. There would be no more plying of ludicrously indulgent cloths that served no purpose other than to announce one's status. I would no longer have to make insipid trivial conversation with other traders either.

I took a deep breath as my father said his words. I did not smile as that would have been insolence and as my parent it was still God's desire

24

that I would respect him. He certainly did have my gratitude though as his narrow-mindedness had now set me free from his business. I will always thank him for that.

Chapter Five

It would seem odd that given my expanding spirituality I would explore life in the military but the life of a soldier offered me much in the way of shedding my old life and opening up new ways.

In truth many young men had no choice but to be conscripted to the army. Given Italy was still a collection of independent provinces during my life, there was always potential for much turmoil within close proximity to Assisi. Men my age, just barely out of our youth were requested however many wealthy families could refuse, instead offering money for armour and weapons: expenses which could greatly drain a region's coffers quickly if a campaign was protracted.

This was exactly what my father did when the generals came to our home.

"You have many sons, you can spare at least two."

It was not so much a request as a demand, and the soldiers knew that more sons could also mean more money if not one was to join them. My father knew this also and was quick to negotiate a more than ample donation to ensure our safety.

I am still not sure what made me speak up that day. There was something romantic in the idea of travelling even a small way from home: it was a wonderful excuse to escape my family and what I felt was the dreariness of Assisi. I was also seduced by the idea of fighting a cause for a justice that I barely understood. In the end I simply attribute it to my naivety.

When I proclaimed that I was willing to serve our army, my father barely protested. I was of minimal use to his business and his wish to have me stay home would have been to appease my mother. Still there was an ache in him that the saving of his money did not smooth over.

"Are you sure?" he asked me.

When I nodded, he too nodded in response. "Perhaps this is what you need to truly become a man."

My training was a wonderful time of learning swordplay and archery. It turned out that I was more suited to being a swordsman. I loved how I felt my body in a whole new way as I jumped and spun around while wielding the huge iron weapon. My muscles grew taut and my skin tightened over them. It was though the exterior of me was now transforming as much as I had within.

27

"Are you ready to kill another with that sword?" one of my generals asked of me one day as I finished slashing at a sack filled with potatoes.

I stopped and looked at the sack as he said this, then tried to imagine it was a man lying bleeding and uttering his final groans as his life escaped his body. In that moment as I held my sword I felt my answer.

"Yes. If it is for good and for justice," I said and squared my jaw.

The general laughed. "I hope you realise that is what the man who will try to gut you with his blade will believe he is doing also. Just remember, he will have the same conviction and dedication to the swing of his weapon. It will be the man who wields his sword the strongest who wins, not the one whose devotion to the cause is the strongest."

I stood for a moment and considered this. Devotion and strength could not be so removed from one another that one could outweigh the other. Surely they must feed one another and in doing so, in becoming blended, make each other even greater.

I said nothing more and simply nodded to my tutor.

As it was, my leaders decided I would not be one of those who would be placed in direct combat. It seems my skills with the sword were nowhere near the expertise that would make me a soldier of any regard.

"You rich boys never make good soldiers," I was told by a surly captain. "Give me a farmer's son who has pushed a barrow or steered an ox since he could walk over you soft-spined thinkers any day."

I was a bit taken aback at first, given my rather overrated self-assessment. However on that first day when I saw our wounded carried back to camp I was thankful to God for keeping me far from the front line. Instead I was reserved as an assistant to the generals; drawing up maps or writing messages to be sent back to Assisi.

"Farmer's sons may have stronger muscles, but you wealthy can at least read and write," a general told me. "Be thankful for the education your family afforded you always."

I truly was. War is brutal. More brutal than you can ever imagine. Even with your modern movies and news coverage, you cannot truly comprehend it until you are there immersed in the smells, sounds and ceaseless tension.

You never rest at all; emotionally, physically or mentally. You have to keep your guard up at all times. You needed to be ready to be summoned even in the depths of night, so that you never slept completely at all. You become exhausted, malnourished due to the lack of fresh food and you face parts of yourself that you never imagined existed.

It was on the worst day of our campaign thus far that I felt Christ closer than ever. It is not so hard to imagine we call upon our gods in harsh times to save us and make us safe, but this was something different. I was standing amongst the wounded and dying at our camp having been sent to make a tally of those unable to fight, and worse still to name the dead in order to send a condolence message to their families.

I walked the rows of the men upon the ground, trying to distinguish faces from beneath the blood and dirt upon them, when the smells of their bodies overwhelmed me. I quickly made way to the edge of the make-shift hospital to gather myself and stop from vomiting. I was taking deep breaths to settle myself and be composed enough to continue my duties, but as I did so I felt the scene before me shift.

It was though I was no longer there but watching from another place entirely, almost like it was a painting before me that had come to life. I was no longer part of it, but simply an observer. It was then I saw him, a perfect likeness of Christ walking amongst the men.

He was not sad or concerned. Instead Jesus walked looking down upon each man with a smile that radiated pure love. For some he stopped and gently caressed their shoulder or brow. Others he would pause by their side and simply place his hand upon his heart. Not once did he look at me, even though I so wanted him to. I knew his presence was for those who needed it in this moment.

Then as quickly as he had appeared Jesus simply walked off into the distance. Once more I became part of the moment, and the sounds and smells enveloped me.

I lay in my bed that night trying to make sense of what I had seen and I heard a voice loud and clear.

"I was what was needed by each man and no more."

I fell asleep pondering this.

It is eternally fascinating to me – both to my being as Saint Francis and beyond how we create situations to serve us, no matter how completely opposite they seem in the actual moment. I know in many lifetimes I created periods of seclusion to go inwards, to truly feel my soul connection and to open parts of me that had been closed off by the mundane routines of life.

It was only a week after my vision that once more I created some solitude in what would be one of the harshest of ways I would ever experience. The soldiers of Perugia who we were battling unleashed their greatest attack thus far. It would be the battle that would end the war and give Assisi its most massive fatality count.

Perugia bought soldiers from other regions to refresh their campaign. This would prove to be an act that would bankrupt them. It would also assign them a rapid and decisive victory which would be seen as enough compensation for such a decision.

The battleground turned into a scene of chaos soon after the attack was launched. Those of us back from the front line could see the wave of enemy bearing down upon us and we knew instantly that our loss was inevitable. Retreat became the only option for those of us not already lost in the fray of swinging swords and flying arrows. We simply turned and ran or rode away.

The retreat was enough of a cry of surrender to the Perugians but they had invested too much into the battle to leave anything to chance. They simply kept ploughing through our men, killing those not quick enough to escape.

We were chased into the surrounding woods like animals; easily bore down upon by the new fresh enemy recruits who were not exhausted or suffering malnutrition. As the woods grew too thick or steep to ride, we made way on foot making our end even more accessible to our hunters.

I heard men scream and utter a final groan as an arrow or sword penetrated them. Behind me I could feel and sense someone getting closer and I was knocked to the ground. I managed to kneel and leant forward, bowing my head, prepared for the sword or dagger that would end it. Instead a foot kicked at my armour.

"This looks new and fancy. How did you pay for this?" the Perugian asked me.

"Just finish him!" a second man snapped.

"I asked you a question!" The first soldier stood before me, grabbed at my chin and pulled my face to look at him.

"My father paid for this," I said.

"You are no farmer's son are you? You speak too pretty for one," he sneered.

I tried to shake my head but his grip was too firm. "No," I said. "My father is a silk merchant."

The soldier smiled and looked to his comrade.

"I think we may have found ourselves a prize here," he said as his grin grew wide.

I was pulled to my feet and had my hands bound behind me. Then each soldier grabbed an arm and began to drag me back towards the battlefield.

As we walked we passed the bodies of my comrades lying in pools of blood. One murmured as we passed and one of the men quickly silenced him with a decisive stab of his sword.

"Some men just don't know when to give up," he laughed.

I saw a few other men from Assisi bound and being escorted. We looked at one another and they were blank stares full of fear and apprehension. Not one of us understood why we had been spared and what was in store for us. However as I looked amongst those who had been captured and not killed I realised why we were of value.

Each one I recognised from Assisi was from my class; these were the sons of the wealthy and educated. Like me most had joined the army for the honour and the adventure. Each soldier the Perugians captured was worth pound upon pound of gold in ransom. We were also the ones who had assisted the officers who had planned the battles and so knew of the strategies of our commanders. Together we were like a treasure chest for Perugia.

We were walked back through the battlefield where the victors were collecting their spoils, ensuring the deaths of the fallen and attending their own wounded. I will never forget what that smelt like nor the sounds a man mortally wounded makes.

I looked about the dead and injured. The blood ran so thick it was like it had been raining. There were vacant eyes everywhere and not just upon the dead. The Perugians moved in silence and I realised that these men sent to finalise the battle were not the commanders and officers or even the hired men but the simple conscripts of their region.

They wandered through the chaos like empty shells. I saw one grimace at the smell and begin to heave. There was no celebration of victory for these men, just relief that they had survived.

Along with the other hostages we were pushed upon carts also being used for armoury and other supplies. I was made to sit upon bundles of spears and arrows. A rope soon secured our hands to the sides of the cart to make it certain we did not attempt any escape during our transfer back to Perugia.

We tried to not make any eye contact with each other as we had been trained to do if captured.

"Say little, do little. Save your strength and resources to plan your escape," was about all that we had been told actually.

There was much wisdom in this though. It did not reveal too much of our knowledge or any emotional weakness that could be exploited. Instead it made us seem like we were worth as little as possible. All they had to measure us upon was our appearance, which for most of us was that of a well-dressed soldier indicating some wealth.

As the cart began to move, one of my two fellow passengers spoke.

"At least we are alive," he muttered.

"I would rather have had my throat cut," hissed the other.

That admission revealed what we were all fearing. Were we being taken for a more barbaric death to entertain the Perugians as they celebrated their victory? Or worse, were we to be tortured for more information?

Neither was to be the case. Instead we were simply to become pawns for Perugia to refill their coffers and re-establish the wealth they had lost in fighting us.

# CHAPTER SIX

We were taken to a town called Collestrada and once there were imprisoned within a cellblock upon the grounds of the army barracks. There we were stripped of our armour and finery. We were given a plain grey tunic and placed into our own separate narrow cell. The walls were thick stone and seemed to be eternally dank and moist. Water even seeped at some of the joins between the huge blocks that surrounded us. There was no window and therefore no light other than a small glow from the torches in the corridor outside our cells. This made its way through a barred opening barely the width and height of a man's hand.

It was quite obvious that escape was futile. The walls could never be breached and getting past the door would only mean confronting whatever amount of guards that would be waiting. Besides we were shackled to a huge pin that was centred at the far wall facing the door. There was enough chain to move and take a few steps. You could manoeuvre to squat over the bucket provided for your waste, but it stopped you short of the door.

Most of my time was spent sitting with my back against the wall as I faced the door, watching that small square of light as it was my only connection to the outside world. I no longer had the sun nor the moon to measure time. I couldn't even feel the cool of night and use this as a marker. All I had was the constant glow of the torches and the eternal damp.

The only change to this was the arrival of a skin of water with barely enough to quench your thirst and a plate of dry bread with some scrap of accompaniment. This happened twice a day at what I imagined was dawn and dusk. Along with this we would have our bucket exchanged for one that was empty. It was a mundane routine but one that at least provided us with some stability.

Now to most of you that would seem a bizarre perspective but I believe that helped keep me sane. I could hear my fellow prisoners sometimes call out for mercy only to receive some punishment for their cries, which invariably then had them yelling in pain. Sometimes I would hear the low murmurs of a prayer and I would join in quietly until our doors were thumped upon by a guard demanding our silence along with a threat.

One night I heard one of the prisoners begin to sing. It was a song of such melancholy that tears filled my eyes. Within his melody I felt his despair and anguish even more than any of the screams for clemency that some resorted to.

I sat down and curled my knees up against my stomach. I wrapped my arms around my legs, rested my head upon my knees and began to cry. They were tears for myself, for my fellow prisoners and for the total stupidity of the war that had placed us here. I fell into my misery with complete relief.

Within those tears I allowed my anguish, my fears and my anger at my imprisonment to rise up and be released. My body may have been shackled but my emotions never would be. They could beat me, tie me tighter, extinguish that one speck of light and make my meals even smaller, but my heart and soul would never be contained.

I fell asleep as I finished crying and remained in that position until I was woken by the guard opening the door to throw in my plate and water. I looked at it and was not even hungry or thirsty. Instead I ate and drank purely to keep myself alive to see the day when I would walk free.

As I ate I took deep breaths and realised something had changed within me as I had slept. There was no more turmoil of thoughts that I had allowed in the days since I had been captured. I no longer wondered what was going to happen. I ceased to fear the sound of the guard's footsteps outside my door. I did not speculate on what had become of my family.

Instead a peace had settled over me that remains hard to describe. It was as though my mind had been wiped clean, but even more it was like I could see, hear and smell differently, opening up a new way for me to be in my cell.

I did not see the walls as confining but protective. I did not wish for more food but was grateful for what I was given. I did not miss my family or home but now saw the blessing of being free from them.

I finished my meal and sat back against the wall. I closed my eyes and took the deepest breath. The smells of my waste bucket and the rotten constant damp did not even make way to my nostrils. Instead I felt a warmth rush through me and in an instant I knew its energy.

It was the Holy Spirit that had been gifted to me and in that moment it overwhelmed me so that I felt I may collapse into tears again. Indeed some made way down my face but they were few. I took another deep breath and felt a presence before me. When I opened my eyes a perfect image of Jesus was before me.

He said nothing but held out his open hands to me. They were empty but I felt their warmth and they glowed with a gentle light.

Jesus then nodded and I knew what his message was without any words. I now understood the blessing of my imprisonment.

I had heard of many sages and wise men who took retreat to converse with God. I even did this in my own way in the mountains around

Assisi, albeit for only an hour or so before returning to the comfort of my home. Now it could be my choice to see this time as an opportunity to be in retreat and not a prisoner. This could be my time to become closer to God.

This is how the control of my captors served me. I was happy to be quiet and thankful for their routine. This allowed me to keep my discipline in its own momentum.

The morning meal was the beginning of my prayers and meditation. The evening meal marked my time to rest and sleep. I never faulted upon this schedule once I began.

Days, weeks and months blended. I stopped counting days as measuring the passage of time as this way no longer served me. All I knew was to wake, eat and pray, then to eat and sleep. It was my saviour, especially when I heard others being released while it seemed my father would not meet the ransom demands. I didn't care, even when the guards chose to tease and taunt me.

"Seems your father does not think you are so valuable," one said to me.

I did not respond, instead offering a silent prayer that his judgement at death would be merciful.

Each time I prayed I felt my words go to God even quicker and the distance not to be so far. Each time I sat in silence I felt the Holy Spirit enter me with more ease and remain for longer. Each moment I chose to give to God was a moment of grace that would set me free. In return I knew God would protect and reward me with perfect timing.

My beard grew long as did the hair upon my head. My prison tunic became rank and my skin was coarse from not bathing. My muscles grew thin and weak. I felt and saw my bones protrude where once my ample flesh had cloaked them. Not once did any of this weigh upon me or make me question my faith. I imagined the saints and prophets before me who had suffered and not let their service to God falter, and though I never imagined my story would equal theirs it gave me resolve to continue.

Each part of my experience was just an opportunity to serve my creator. When I woke I thanked him for being alive. I offered prayers to the men who orchestrated the war. I blessed my body for surviving. I began to smile at the guards and thank them when they gave me a meal.

"That one has finally cracked," I heard one say as he shut my door.

Indeed the few who were left within the cells had found their own solace in escaping the harshness of our reality. One paced all day and recited history. Another simply begged all day to be killed. I believe he stopped eating to do so himself. The threats from the guards stopped as they too had grown weary of trying to discipline us.

Some may say I had found my own escape. That this spiritual endeavour was simply to help me survive and I would agree. However I had a clarity that was beyond the simple mechanism of survival. My "escape" was founded in truth and balance. I was not defeated. I was grounded in trust that my imprisonment was simply a passing event, even when the months continued to add themselves to my time.

To me this was an investment in my soul. I was not just finding a way to fill each day and keep my mind occupied lest it be lost to insanity or despair. I was creating a foundation for a life with God so close that I would never be led astray again. I would never choose a path that would keep me from grace and honour.

This time to me was like being given a key to the kingdom of heaven, and once I knew how to open it, God would show me the way forevermore. I also knew that I would be there as prisoner until my Lord knew I was ready to walk the Earth with a full heart and a noble spirit. So I did not feel hate for the fact that my father had not met the demands for months upon end. I simply knew I was not ready to be free yet.

CHAPTER SEVEN

It was almost a year after my capture that my cell door was opened only an hour or so after my morning meal. I was deep in prayer and not expecting this so that I did not notice until the guard muttered to me.

"Get on your feet."

I stood, very slowly using the wall to help me. This was how I had to stand now in my weakened state. I kept my eyes down and placed my hands in each other. When nothing seemed to happen I looked up and saw the guard still in the doorway. He turned to call out to another.

"Come and help me!"

A second man appeared and looked at me.

"What do you think he could possibly do to you? He is skin and bones. If you pushed him he would break in two!"

"I don't care. Just come and hold his hands while I undo the shackle," was his response.

He moved forward and began to kneel while the second guard grabbed my wrists almost tentatively. As he did so he looked into my eyes.

"You're going home," he said plainly just as the shackle was opened and thrown behind me.

I looked down and for the first time in a year my leg was free from the metal clamp and chain. The skin beneath it was red and scarred but I felt nothing. Then the guard let go of my hands and let them drop by my side.

"Come on. As soon as you get back on that cart I can go and do some real work," snarled the first guard.

One man walked before me and the other behind. My feet seemed so heavy, barely used to walking at all anymore. I stepped to the place that my chain would have stopped and I instantly halted, as though I could not believe that I could go further.

A quick shove and grunt from my surly guard was all that was needed to overcome this and I was soon through the doorway and within the corridor. As I walked past the other cells I could see they were open and empty. I was the last to be set free or survive. I did not ponder upon this at all though.

If making way past the bounds of my chain had seemed a challenge it was nothing compared to finally be outside and in the open. I was completely overwhelmed: firstly by the sunlight which felt it would both burn and blind me. I put my hands to my face immediately to protect my eyes.

"Yes that would be a shock wouldn't it? Take a moment or else you won't be able to see to walk," I heard from a voice nearby. It was not the voice of either guard but a new one entirely.

In that moment I felt my body taken by the heat of the day. Then another wave of sensations hit me as the sounds and smells of everything around came rushing to me.

I could hear birds singing, the calls of soldiers in the distance, the smells from a nearby kitchen layered upon those of the plants around me. My feet were upon grass that almost felt irritating after so long upon cold stone. I was completely lost within each sensation that seemed to besiege me so I could not even find the sense to pray.

Not until I collapsed upon my knees and then I called out to God. "Help me Lord!"

I am not sure if it was seconds or minutes but no one approached or said anything to me. As I knelt upon the ground praying for the deluge upon my body to stop I heard God clearly.

"Fear not the blessing I have bestowed upon you."

I immediately understood. This was not a weakness I had developed but strength. I had now opened my senses beyond those of a normal man. I smiled as I let this seep into my awareness and suddenly my surrounds did not seem so harsh. I opened my eyes and looked directly to the sun.

"Well it seems the Lord has helped you recover," the third guard said and laughed as he reached for my elbow to pull me up. "How about he comes and helps you bathe."

It was a cursory bath I was offered; just enough to wash off the stench and no more. My skin was still left rough and some parts still had smears of dirt. My hair was hacked to a reasonable length and my beard was clipped close to my face. A fresh tunic was thrown on me and some simple sandals that felt odd upon my feet after them being bare so long.

I smiled as I looked down upon my new clothing. It was simple wool and yet it felt like the finest silk. It made me think of my father's textiles and the clothes I used to wear. That life seemed so far away from me now, almost like it had never existed. Now as I sat upon the cart again, bouncing heavily upon the road back to Assisi, I had to consider what it would be like to return to that life.

A cold shiver actually passed through me as I imagined walking back into my family home and seeing my parents. I pictured the opulent furniture, the excessive meals and the behaviour they would expect I return to.

I lowered my head and prayed. My connection to God would show me the way. I did not need to think about what to say or do. God would guide me.

When the cart arrived in Assisi it was met by our local soldiers. I was handed over with little pomp or ceremony.

"Who do you have?"

"Francisco di Bernardone."

And with that I was once more a free resident of Assisi.

Another short cart ride took me to my home. When the cart stopped I looked and for a moment thought it was the wrong house. It was not quite how I remembered it. A servant opened the door. They were obviously expecting me.

One of the Assisi soldiers who had escorted me jumped down from the cart and gestured for me to do so also. As I began to awkwardly lower myself he came forward to help me.

"No!" I cried and he stepped back hesitantly.

I was soon upon the ground and though my feet felt solid, I could feel my legs shake a little. The soldier once more put out his hand to help me but I ignored it and made my first step forward. Each step made the house bigger and the thoughts of what faced me inside of it even larger. I looked up at the windows with their fancy curtains and the ornate woodwork that framed them.

"This is just another prison," I thought and yet I still made my way to its door.

When I stepped inside there was just the one servant to greet me.

"Good day, Sir," she said quietly not looking me in the eye. "We will wash and dress you, then your family will greet you."

She nodded to the soldier who returned the gesture with a bow and then he turned to leave. Two of our male butlers came into the hallway now and one stepped forward.

"Welcome home, Sir. Let us take you to bathe," he said simply.

I was not led to the bathroom upstairs amongst the bedrooms. I was led into the laundry room that was behind the house. A laugh rose up within me when I realised where I was being taken.

"So I need to be scrubbed clean like a dirty dish before I can be seen or truly welcomed home," I tried to say loudly through my laugh, certain my family was close enough to hear. My voice though was raspy and unclear from so many months without any true conversation. The servants ahead of me barely heard what I said.

"Pardon Sir," one stopped and turned to me.

39

"It is of no consequence," I replied and we continued on to the laundry room.

An old tub was made ready for me with warm water and some oils. As I lowered myself into it, the comfort of its embrace almost felt the opposite. It was as though I was being pulled back into this world of opulence that I no longer felt a part of.

"I imagine we will be turning this into cleaning cloths," one of the servants joked as he held up my tunic.

I looked at it and shook my head.

"No, I should like to keep that," I said.

My words were said with no emotion and for a moment the servant looked at my face in the hope that I may smile as some indication that I was joking. When he soon realised I was far from any humour, he placed the tunic upon a pile of other clothes that were waiting to be washed.

"As you wish Sir," he said as he did this.

With my bath over and my skin once more smooth and completely clean, my hair was trimmed and my beard shaved off. Then it was time to be dressed. Cotton undergarments were then layered with pants, a shirt and a coat. Socks and shoes were wrapped around my feet. Oils were dabbed through my hair and upon my face.

I was once more the acceptable sight and scent of an Assisi noble-man. However as I looked down upon my body all I could see and feel was confinement.

I was escorted back into the main house and the female servant was once more expecting me.

"Your family are waiting in the parlour," she said and gestured towards the door that was open but only slightly.

I took a deep breath and walked towards it, slowly pushing the door open wide enough to step through. As I did I revealed my family. My mother was seated upon her usual chair while my father stood to her side. My sisters were upon couches and seats around the room, and my brothers stood behind them.

I could not help but smile as I imagined my father arranging them into position so that this reunion would be as formal as possible. My smile though was not seen as mocking by my family. They saw it as an understated relief to once more be in their presence and within my home.

"Oh Francisco!" my mother whimpered and put her hand to her mouth as she sat forward in her chair. My father gently pushed her back and she immediately composed herself.

My father simply nodded but his expression said much more. It was matched by the faces of each person within the room. They looked shocked and uncomfortable, as though someone entirely different to their child or sibling was standing before them.

"You are so thin."

It was my sister Elisabetta who finally spoke, though her voice was barely above a whisper. My brother Paolo shook his head and looked down.

"I am grateful to be alive and free," was all I could feel to say.

It was little consolation to those before me. They had argued with my father to meet the demands sooner. Now standing before them with my skin hanging on my bones and my eyes sunken into my face they were confronted with the reality of my imprisonment. This made all they had imagined expand into even greater guilt and sympathy. I was now grateful I had been bathed, groomed and dressed before they saw me.

"Let us go and eat," my mother said.

"It is too early," I said plainly, my body still locked into its prison routine.

"I do not care. I will see you eat and we shall truly have you home once you have sat at the dining table."

With that she rose from her chair and took my hand. Behind her I saw my father remain in position as stoic as ever. Not one of my siblings dared move until he finally did, following my mother and I out of the room.

We sat quickly within our usual chairs, once our parents had taken theirs. My mother watched me and smiled as I sat down. Then looked amongst all her children.

"Let us thank God to have our table full once more," she said and tears fell down her cheek.

I immediately put my hands together and said the prayer I always did when my meal had been bought to me in my cell. When I finished and looked up, all eyes were upon me.

"Where did you learn those words?" my sister Angelina asked me.

I stopped for a moment. I hadn't even realised I had created my own prayer to give thanks and bless my meal.

"It is a prayer I would say when my meal was bought to me," I answered.

"It is glorious," said my mother and smiled.

The meal unfolded with much small talk. I was updated on the local gossip, filled in on the family's current business and informed of all the recent betrothals that had been enacted or awaiting their wedding day; the most recent being that of my sister Lucia.

"We wanted to wait for your return. It will be next month now," my mother said as Lucia blushed a deep shade of scarlet.

Life had continued on and would continue to do so upon my return. I tried to smile and relate to all that they spoke of but it seemed distant and inconsequential. What they shared seemed to be so important to the one speaking of it, and yet to me it was as though they were reading a story from a book.

I looked at every one of them in turn. Each of my siblings was a person deeply connected to me. We shared the same parents, had grown together and knew each other's secrets and habits. Yet they were almost like strangers. Even my mother with her smiles, tears and questions of concern did not evoke any bond within me.

Suffice to say I had reached this point many years before with my father. I did not look upon him once as we ate and I am sure he avoided looking at me. He ate in silence, tolerating the trivial conversation and thankful that I was not being asked any details about my imprisonment. Frankly that was seen as something far too delicate to address at the dinner table and so soon. In fact it was something that would never be asked of me by anyone, and that was well chosen by them as no one would have benefited by that sharing.

I picked at my meal, hardly able to eat any of it. In fact what had been placed before me was equal to what I would have eaten in almost a week whilst in prison. Even eating a small amount of such rich food made my stomach seem to churn as it tried to deal with the heaviness after so long on so much less. I sat back in my chair and placed my hand upon my stomach, then closed my eyes as I felt my insides adjusting.

"Would you like to rest now?" my mother asked and all I could do was nod.

Lying once more upon my bed, my body rejoiced at the softness and the warmth below and around me. I fell quickly into the deepest sleep I could ever recall. If I did dream, there was no memory of it. I did not even hear when my brother Pietro came into the room to take to his bed.

CHAPTER EIGHT

I woke suddenly in the very early hours of the morning. It was yet dark and the moonlight broke through a gap in the curtains, drawing a white line across the room. The bed no longer felt comforting but as though it might never release me, so I pulled myself up and walked to the window.

Drawing the curtains apart I let the moon send even more of her light into the room as I stood in awe of her beauty. It had been so long since I had seen the night sky that I had forgotten how gentle and graceful it could be.

Behind me Pietro stayed undisturbed and his breathing was in a steady rhythm. I felt the calm tempo of my own breath and closed my eyes. Then the gratitude I had for my life consumed me.

"My Lord, thank you for my safe return. Thank you for allowing me this moment after all those before it. I will continue to serve you. I will continue to embrace the Holy Spirit and make my life worthy."

I then knelt on the floor and continued my prayers. This was how Pietro found me in the morning.

"How long have you been awake?" he asked.

"I do not know," I answered honestly.

Looking up for the first time since I had begun praying I could see that the sun was up and the sky was no longer black. I figured it had been at least three hours or so. I lowered my head and continued my prayers as Pietro dressed and left the room.

Eventually a maid came looking for me.

"Sir, breakfast is ready," she called through the opening in the doorway.

I smiled and almost laughed when I realised I had been waiting for a dish to be pushed before me. It had been an entire day since my release and yet I was still locked into my old patterns. I called out in response, then dressed myself and made way to the dining room.

There was no one there except Lucia. All others had finished and were about their daily work or duties. Lucia looked up and smiled.

"Did you sleep well?" she asked awkwardly but with sincerity to begin conversation.

"Yes I did. As you can imagine it was the most pleasant sleep I have had in some time," I responded.

"As it was for us all to have you home finally," she said.

We then ate in silence until Lucia put down her fork and rose from her seat.

"I must make way. As you can imagine I have much to plan for the wedding," she informed me and her cheeks blushed as they always would when she talked about her impending marriage.

I too was finished eating but unlike all the others I had nothing to beckon me or give me need to leave the table. I sat back in my chair as servants came in and began to clear the table. I thought about going back to my room and praying through the day but I knew I could not turn my bedroom into another cell. I would have to head outside some time and the sooner the better.

Walking out the front door, I stopped and looked left and then right. To the right I would head into the town centre. There I would come across all those people I had left behind. They would look upon me, wondering what I had endured, what sort of person I now was and there would be an endless flow of questions to satisfy their curiosity as well as trivial conversation to fill the time.

To my left I could walk and soon be within the hills around Assisi. I might come across a shepherd, or a farmer as I walked. They would not know my name, nor would they have any questions. They would offer a smile and a greeting, then we would continue on our way. Then I could find a quiet place with the beauty of the land around me, and there I would pray.

I turned to my left and made my way.

As I walked the sun grew stronger and warmer. My coat grew heavier and a burden. So I took it off, draping it upon the branch of a tree with the intention of collecting it upon my return. Even without it I was still warm and reached to undo the collar of my shirt, and then roll up my sleeves. I was tempted to peel off my trousers but resisted, deciding to keep some level of societal decency.

I soon found a delightful space to make my retreat for the day. There was a lovely clearing that offered me enough height to feel isolated and gave me a glorious view. A large olive tree was anchored into the ground behind me, throwing forward its branches to give me some respite from the strong sun. A cool breeze danced in front of me, occasionally kissing my feet and legs.

A deep sigh made way from inside of me. Now I felt free.

The routine of my prison life was now replaced with the routine of my visiting the hillsides each day. It might seem I was creating some sort of comfort to fill a void but it was so different. Daily habits are not always about control and limitations. They can be created in love and honour. Then they become so much more.

This was how I transformed my time imprisoned in Perugia. Though I was locked up, and had restrictions upon me, I took that which had been imposed and infused it with what would touch my heart and give me some joy. Any joy is better than none and it can be found in the darkest of times and situations.

Now with my freedom and the beauty of the countryside I could create in an even grander way. I did not walk from my home each day in blind servitude to my prayers and longing to connect with God. I did so as it made my heart sing. It made me feel something so grand that I still can barely describe it.

When discipline comes from a deep desire, from a passion that cannot be compromised, then it is not a form of penance. It becomes your life breath. It becomes the drive to continue on and know more. It is the fuel that keeps your fire alive.

Each time I woke and wondered where I would pray that day, I knew that I was also going to be gifting myself more of my connection to God. Not once did that seem like a chore or a burden to me. Not once did I consider to just stay within my bed, or upon the couches which filled my home. I knew I would not be satisfied until I was sitting in silence with just the whispers of the trees around me.

I took no wine or food with me. That was another blessing of my time in prison; I had let go of the need for such things other than what was truly needed to sustain me. All I had with me was my breath, my heartbeat and the glorious sense of my Lord with me. It was all I needed.

As you can imagine my daily excursions did not go unnoticed by my family. I would be welcomed home in the evenings with polite nods but I would also see the sideways glances and hear the mutterings. None of this affected me at all. I could not conform to the way of life that they had all accepted, and the more I connected with the Lord and Holy Spirit the more I knew the old life of my family could never be that of mine.

Thankfully my father now considered me "effected". This was the polite term given to a member of a noble family who had a mental illness. My lack of conformity saw me fit to be labelled as such and while it was never said in my presence, I knew it was said nonetheless. This situation suited me perfectly as it had released me from the expectations of a society that I no longer felt a part of.

My father though still believed that I would outgrow such a state. He looked around at other men who had come back from battle or imprisonment and saw them return to the normality of life that had been assigned them before. I will grant him that he did have some patience with me that had never been shown to me or any of my siblings before. This patience though was wearing thin and he began to spit barbs at me.

"Off for another walk?" he would sneer as I left the house.

I would nod and continue on my way while behind me I would hear him add, "Well it must be nice to not have to work."

You could imagine that such taunts, along with the other gestures of those around me would eventually have irritated or angered me. They did no such thing to my state of being at all. In fact it only made my resolve to connect with spirit even stronger. A quip or an eye-roll only earned that person some prayers from me to ask that they would find their way to God.

I did explain that my days were spent in prayer and soulful communion with our Lord but this was met with everything ranging from disbelief to scornful judgement.

"Then surely you could do so within the church?" snapped my father.

That could not be at all. My father spoke with his understanding of what that building stood for along with the men who plied its trade. I did attend Sunday Mass from a place of respect and honour for its tradition and blessings it could offer. While there I saw the congregation were gathered in the hope of the salvation and redemption which they all needed. I however did not seek either.

I was no longer lost or confused. I did not see God as an elusive being that I would only reach through our priests. In that moment when I gave my life to our Lord with absolute trust for whatever that would create for me I had set myself free. There is no need of deliverance for a free man. There is no need to have anything explained.

I had set myself free from the constraints of society. I was no longer clouded by the expectations that conforming placed upon men. I did not need anyone to guide me to God. That moment in my cell when I offered my life to God and felt the Holy Spirit flow through me I became a clear conduit for his work and his teachings. That this now made me "crazy" was of no consequence to the greater good that I knew my life was serving.

My resolve needed no confirmation or signs. I lived in inherent trust of all that I had become. So that day when I stood within the ruins of a church on the outskirts of Assisi and I heard my Lord say so clearly,

"My son, rebuild my church."

I knew with all my heart this was not just a request to repair the dilapidated shell I stood within. I felt beyond the immediate words he shared. This broken-down shrine was a symbol for what the church had become. Its truth and glory had been abandoned. There was no joy or hope within any of its walls. Its men were lost and hollow.

I nodded and smiled.

"Yes my Lord."

Then I felt hesitation within me.

"But how?" I asked. "Guide me."

I felt a warmth flow through me and once more I knew the Holy Spirit was within me.

"I will always guide you. I will never abandon you. Begin where you are in this moment," was the reply I felt like the embrace of an angel.

With that I looked around me, then began to clear out the debris within the church.

I had little means or expertise to rebuild the actual building I had found that day but did what I was capable of, knowing that would be more than enough. Its roof was intact but barely. Its windows were cracked and dust was layered upon the floor and what remained of its pews and altar. Outside the gardens lived on without the guidance of a gardener so they now were tall and encroached upon the building. Plants pushed into the doorways and through the damaged windows.

I cleared the dust and wiped the furniture clean. Though I loved the rambling garden I cleared it from the entrance-ways and pushed back the fronds and stems that poked in the windows. I gathered what I could from my home to close off the windows that were missing glass. Sometimes this was with some wood but I also took some of the precious cloths that my father sold.

The front doors were jammed shut and I worked upon them until they could once again swing open. When I did this it let the most glorious blast of sunshine into the small chapel. The stream fell upon the altar like a presence much grander than the simple daylight that it was and I felt the Lord once more claim this place for his presence and teachings.

"Come stand with me," he beckoned and I walked to stand behind the altar and look upon the church.

It was only ten pews deep, and each side would have only sat four to five people each. Its small size had made it redundant as the main cathedral in Assisi had grown. Now as I stood here I saw it as reborn and with that rebirth it would also allow a new way to guide people to God.

I heard a noise above me and I looked up to the right. There I saw a small bird had made a nest where the beams from the ceiling met the wall. She had small babies and they were calling out to her. My first thought was that I had no ladder to reach and clear the nest. Then I paused

47

and I knew this too was a lesson from God.

There was no need to remove the nest. The bird and her babies were more than welcome within God's house, as would be any creature, great or small, who made their way here. God would never deny anyone who found their way to him and neither would I deny anyone who found their way to this chapel.

I looked back down the aisle and out the doorway, then back amongst the empty chairs. I began to laugh.

"Now what shall I do?" I laughed as I said this out loud.

And the answer I received was just as loud and filled with joy.

"Begin!" I heard.

So I did.

There was no other human within the church but I spoke as though there were a hundred. I spoke about the joy of connecting with God, of the delight of feeling the Holy Spirit fill me and the freedom of knowing your life is within God's hands. When I felt complete with this, I went before the altar, knelt down and began to pray.

CHAPTER NINE

This became my new life, so much so that now I did not even return to my family home. My church of San Damiano became my dwelling. There was a small room to the side of the altar that once would have been the place the residing priest would have made himself ready, where candles and incense would be stored. This had been long emptied and was where I now resided.

It was just a few feet wider and longer than my prison cell had been. Thankfully it differed in many other ways as well. Though it had stone walls, they were not wet and dank. I had a window to let in light and fresh air, and gathered some blankets from home to make a mattress to sleep upon.

I would forage for food, gathering greens from the hillside and fruit from trees that grew wild. A walk to the river gave me water and somewhere to bathe. My surrounds always provided me with all that I needed and not once did I have to beg or steal for my food. I will admit that there were times that I would have wanted for some bread or cheese, and these too came to me in other ways eventually.

My family accepted that I was gone and though it only fed the story that I was insane, there was a certain relief within the household.

"He will come back," my mother insisted but my father would snort and think about the money he had wasted on my ransom.

The situation may have stayed this way until I died but then things began to change just as I imagined they would.

I was standing behind the altar one day giving my sermon for the day. If my memory serves me I was talking about the crucifixion of Jesus. My hands were raised in the air and I was looking to the heavens. Then as I looked back down I saw the silhouette of someone standing in the open doorway at the front of the church.

I paused and blinked, wondering if I was seeing someone real or if this was a heavenly visitation. The shadow shifted and stepped forward and I could now see it was a young man, about my age. He was dressed simply: neither a nobleman nor a peasant. I could tell he had been listening intently.

"Sorry, I didn't mean to interrupt. Might I stay and listen?" he asked and continued to walk in before my answer.

"Of course," I said and gestured to the front pew. Then I continued on with the first member of my congregation.

Sabatino was a traveller and this was a rare thing in our time. People seldom travelled for the experience of travelling. They were either doing business or they were on their way to family. Sabatino was in fact from a very noble family in the north. He would simply fill a purse and travel until he only had enough money to return back home. Then he would refill it and head in another direction.

"It has its limits, but nowhere near as limiting as being in one place," he told me.

Sabatino dressed simply so as not to gain attention or curiosity as to how much his purse may contain. "It also helps me acquire more reasonable prices!" he exclaimed as people did not expect he would have the finances to allow being over-charged.

As he travelled into new regions or sailed to an unfamiliar destination, Sabatino had found something within him open up. He looked at people differently and wanted to know more about them. New places and new ways had shown Sabatino he too could become a different man.

"If we simply let our home and family define us, then how do we become the best we can be? Yes, I am sure we become the best our home and family believe we can be, but what if there is more?"

Sabatino was making his way into Assisi when he had seen the small chapel and it had intrigued him, as did all "ruins" or as he called them "pieces of history" that he passed. As he walked closer he heard my voice and became even more curious.

"I felt like I was intruding at first but then there was something you said that just grabbed at my heart."

Sabatino never could remember exactly what that was and in truth it did not matter. He left soon after I finished my talk but returned the next day, a bit earlier this time in the hope he would hear my entire sermon. The day after that he was also there when I opened the doors. The day after this he was waiting again but this time there was another man standing beside him.

"I was telling Morico about you at the tavern last night and he wanted to come and hear you also."

So my congregation grew to two, but it did not stop there. A week later a nearby farmer followed Sabatino and Morico to see what they were doing, and then he remained. The farmer returned the next day with some fresh baked bread.

"You need to offer us communion," he said as he handed it to me, and so I did.

I soon had other farmers join us, stating it was far easier than to go into town. Indeed many of them would not attend the main town mass for that reason. I was now providing them with not only a practical alternative but one in which fellow parishioners did not look down upon them for how they dressed or their state of hygiene. When they first came they sat at the back pews as they would have in any cathedral but within days they would be at the front, embracing the words of our Lord with no shame of their occupation or appearance.

Sabatino said his farewell one day. "I need to make way home but will return," he said and I knew this would be true.

He returned one month later, with five other travellers he collected upon the way, and before him he pushed a barrow with the most wonderful gift; a solid brass bell.

"Call the people! Let them know you are here!" he said and smiled.

We cut some small trees and made a frame beside the church, then set the bell up high. A rope provided by one of the farmers finished it off. The bell was not so large, yet somehow when I first pulled upon that rope it sounded louder than Gabriel's trumpet.

Yes, it declared what I was doing. Yes, it summoned even more people to my doors. What it also did was earn the ire of the priests in Assisi. Word had already made its way to the cathedral but the stories had been dismissed.

"Let him gather the strangers and the misfits. We have more than enough work serving the nobility within the town," one elder priest said.

However when many of the young men of the town began to make their way, concerns were raised once again.

"They will return," stated the same elder.

But they didn't and the bell continued its call to all around. The small talk became much more and five priests arrived at my father's door.

"Signor di Bernardone, you must take action with your son. You must call him to order. He is defying the laws of the church with his actions. He is leading people astray with his unfettered teaching!"

That was how my father, along with my brothers, Pietro and Michael, came to the church. My father looked about the chapel, and clenched his jaw as he saw fabrics and pieces of furniture that I had taken from his home.

He sat with me upon the front pew, with my brothers behind us and began his lecture. I need not recount the words as they amounted to nothing worth repeating. It was simply requested that I stop my occupation and return home.

"We just want you back with the family," Michael said softly behind me. "We are worried for you."

51

I turned so I could face Michael. "Can you truly look about you and worry for what I am doing? Can you look into my eyes and truly worry for the life I have chosen?"

Michael paused, took a deep breath and shook his head. I am sure Pietro and my father felt that way too but my father's shame at having his family derided would not accept this.

"You will return home," my father said as he stood from his seat. "Or you shall no longer be part of my family."

My father was a man of his word. Honour was not just an expression for him to speak of; it was a code that would be adhered to. One week later a messenger arrived with a summon to appear in the Assisi court. I looked upon the parchment and laughed. Then I saw my father's name upon the paper and I was torn. I knew there was no need for me to follow my father's order yet I still felt obliged to honour him as my parent. That was a law of my Lord set out thousands of years ago.

I held the paper and saw this was not just a legal matter that I must abide by or tempt with my insolence. This was an opportunity for resolution and clarity.

There were two more days before I had to make my way into town and I used this time to pray for guidance and for the completion that I felt this situation offered. I held my mass in the morning and shared what my day held for me. I looked upon the faces of those gathered and I knew this was not just for myself that this was happening. I felt them also remember their own family turmoils, but even more so they saw the challenge of following your soul passion.

How many of them before me had compromised their desires and dreams to fit within their family? How many of them could I guide to their own freedom by staying within my connection to spirit?

As I began to walk into town, Sabatino began to close the doors, but I turned and made him stop.

"The doors stay open until nightfall," I said. "People can pray without me here, and you can offer them communion if they desire."

Sabatino smiled and pulled the doors wide again.

I will admit darkness washed into my chest and down into my belly as I got closer to town. I paused for a moment and felt it. It was the opposite of when the Holy Spirit would flow through me and I knew this heavy feeling was simply all my old fears returning. They had lived with me for so long within this town that they simply felt they could rise again as I walked these streets.

I took a deep breath.

"I am no longer that man. You are free to go," I silently declared and I felt the darkness lift and the warmth of the Holy Spirit reclaimed me. I squared my shoulders and made way to the courthouse.

People nodded politely to me as I passed them, while others looked away to avoid engaging with a madman. Each response amused me in its own way. Thankfully I was soon at the courthouse and was ushered in by one of the magistrate's assistants. My father was already there as were some of the elder priests. They all sat solemnly upon chairs which lined the small room. I remained standing in the centre of the room and looked ahead to the desk at which the magistrate would sit.

He eventually entered the room and took his place, calling my father and myself to stand before him.

"Francisco, you have been called here on petition of your father, that you return to your family home, recommence your familial duties and return his belongings. You shall do so immediately, such that when you leave this courthouse you will go directly to your family home."

It was exactly as I expected. My father had followed through with his threat and executed it in the most exact way that he could. I smiled and delivered my response.

"I shall not," I said simply and calmly, looking straight ahead at the magistrate.

I will admit that I anticipated my father's reaction and he played it out just as I had imagined. He began by throwing his hands in the air.

"You see Sir! You see what I must endure with this child. The petulance and challenges are constant and enduring. He has no respect for me or his family. It is like raising a stranger," he yelled with perfect predictability. Then he threw one more insult. "And yet he is happy to stand there in clothes I paid for and to furnish his house of sins with goods I have earned! In return I am derided and shamed!"

I looked down upon my clothes and remembered how it had felt when I returned home from Perugia and had them placed upon me. I thought about the fabrics and small pieces of furniture in the chapel. Each piece of clothing, cloth and wood kept me tied to my past and kept me in debt and beholden. Immediately I knew the solution.

I pulled off my coat and threw it to the floor. Then my shirt. I grabbed at my shoes and stripped my stockings.

"What are you doing?" cried out the magistrate.

"Returning my father's belongings," I replied as I added my trousers to the pile before me. Soon I stood completely naked and pointed to the clothes while everyone within the room gaped at me incredulously.

"There!" I turned to my father whose face had turned a deep scarlet. "I return what is yours. The furnishings will make way to your home by evening. By daybreak tomorrow I will owe you nothing!"

My father stared down at the clothes and I saw his chest heaving. Then he slowly looked up at me and his eyes were dark and fierce.

"I denounce you! I reject you from my blood! You are no longer my son!" he spat.

I wanted to smile but I could not. Despite being offered the final piece of my freedom from this man, it was so clouded in anger and bitterness that it was hard to embrace in the moment.

He turned to the magistrate. "He is not worthy of my home or my estate. Today he loses all rights to his name and to any inheritance. He is not welcome in my house. He will never be received there again!"

The magistrate looked at me and spoke slowly. "Francisco, do you realise what this means? You have been severed from your family. There will be no option to return or be accepted again."

I slowly nodded, and now I did feign a smile. My past had been truly set free. I had no safety net or any obligations. There was just open possibilities in which to move ahead. Indeed in letting go of my past, all that I had was my future.

My father turned and left, but as he walked through the doorway he stopped and turned to the priests who remained silent in their chairs.

"He is no longer my problem to solve for you. He is now yours to deal with in whatever way you see fit."

That would be the last time I would see or hear my father. He returned home and shared with my mother what had occurred. She immediately collapsed upon the floor in tears, while my father poured himself some wine. He had no remorse or grief to feel. My final rejection of him had just been an insult to his authority. His pride had been wounded and he reacted in what he saw was the perfect way.

In cutting me from the family he could now live in relief. My presence had been like a gangrenous wound that would not heal. With the rotting flesh that I was considered now removed, his family could carry onwards. He would not regret this, not even once.

In the courthouse the priests looked to each other.

"We will discuss this when we return home," one whispered and they all remained silent while the magistrate dealt with me.

"Please, at least put your undergarments back on," he asked of me but I shook my head.

"I will leave here naked before I put any of those back on me," I declared.

"Well we can't allow that!" he snapped and called to one of his assistants.

They fetched me a coarse, brown woollen robe. It was very simple, hanging straight to the ground, with big wide sleeves and a hood that could be pulled over your head in rain or colder weather. A piece of cord made do for a belt. These robes were kept for the homeless and destitute to provide some modesty when their own clothes fell to shreds. A simple pair of sandals; just enough to make walking on the open ground comfortable finished my new ensemble.

"I will return this as soon as I have my own," I said.

The magistrate shook his head emphatically. "No you will not! I do not want to see you within my courthouse again. Go and do—well— whatever it is you are doing in the peaceful way you are doing it."

With that he stood and left the room. I crossed my arms within my sleeves and turned to leave. The priests looked at me blankly and I nodded to them in response, then I made way back to my hillside church.

Sabatino and Morico were waiting for me outside our chapel and they did not realise it was me until I was close enough for them to make out my face.

"What happened to your clothes?" Morico asked.

"A wonderful thing!" I answered.

I took them inside and as I retold the story, we began to gather the few things I had taken from my family home to restore the church. Interestingly it was far less than it had seemed and did not impact the chapel in anyway. One of the farmers took them all upon his cart to return to my father, and as the cart left me I felt the final shreds of connection slip away.

Within days it was all replaced by my congregation, and even more remarkably many began to enact the more involved repairs that I had been unable to do on my own. It was like a rebirth and it felt wonderful, as though everything was evolving and expanding into another stage. I silently thanked my father for his part in this and offered prayers to him.

CHAPTER TEN

In Assisi the priests at the court had walked in silence back to the monastery beside the cathedral in town. They hurried to their salon where other elders and priests were waiting to hear the results.

"Is he returning home?" one asked as they took their seats.

Father Antonio shook his head and the room erupted in gasps and sighs.

"Even worse is that he has been cast from his family. Signor di Bernardone has denounced him and denied him any inheritance. He has no family to answer to. This is now our problem entirely," Antonio explained.

The room fell silent as the priests pondered this.

"I say we ignore him. What harm can he be doing? All he gathers are vagrants, farmers and philosophers," spat Father Henri.

"But he isn't just gathering these. The young men who Francisco studied and drank with are now making their way and soon they will take their families with them! We are starting to lose the nobles as well as the peasants. If we lose the younger nobility all we will be left with is the older generation and as each one dies our congregation grows smaller. In the meanwhile, his will grow," Antonio explained.

Within those words Antonio said so much more. A dwindling congregation meant a dwindling of coins in the offertory which was concerning enough. However a dwindling nobility upon the pews meant a decrease in the larger donations and gifts which truly kept them comfortable.

Not one man disagreed when Antonio offered his solution.

"We will let Rome deal with this."

When the letter from Assisi arrived at the Vatican, the cardinal assigned such issues sighed heavily and rubbed his forehead. It was not the first time that a rogue priest had been reported and it certainly would not be the last. Many a time a priest unsatisfied or dissonant with his fellow priests would leave their parish and begin preaching wherever and however they could.

Usually Rome did not have to do anything about it. By the time the letter reporting them arrived and an investigation began the priest would have calmed down and returned to the parish they had left. Sometimes a simple reassignment settled their discontent. In other instances they would be admitted to a mental institution.

The true rogues, the ones who wanted to teach Christianity in the way they believed, who twisted the teachings and made it truly different were rare. Thankfully. Most commonly they would not gather any followers, or the ones they did were minimal and equally delusional as to the ways of the bible. So when it was reported that I had not only claimed a disused church but was now preaching and gathering a congregation, Cardinal Alessandro knew this would not be a simple case.

To make things worse I was not even a true priest. I had not studied in the seminary. I had not served under any cardinals, bishops or monsignors let alone a common father or brother. What I was teaching would have no structure or guidelines.

"He could be one of those new philosophical teachers who is dredging up the old mysteries which we have shed!" he thought and shuddered.

Alessandro folded up the letter and placed it into his sleeve. He stood from his desk and sighed again as he looked to the crucifix upon his wall.

"Dear Lord, please do not let it be me who they send to question the man!" he quickly prayed and then made his way to the council room.

The council room was as grand as you can imagine. It housed a table long enough to seat thirty men, plus a line of chairs circled the room, meaning one hundred men could sit here and discuss anything needed. It was filled with paintings and tapestries that were centuries old, and between these was elaborate plaster work painted in gold and deep tones of red.

This room had held witness to reformations, power plays and decisions which had begun and ended monastic careers. Today my humble church was discussed for all the council members to hear. Alessandro read out the letter from the Assisi priests and then added his personal concerns.

"He is untrained and therefore even more unpredictable. The rate at which he gathers his congregation suggests he is charismatic and personable, which also makes him a threat to the true teachings as we ascribe them."

"Well then you must go and see what exactly he is doing," said the Cardinal who headed the meeting.

Alessandro cringed inside and his mind snapped to attention. "Sir, this cannot be. The lands around Assisi are still volatile from recent battles. It is not safe for any of us to travel. There are still reports of men being taken hostage."

"No one will touch a Vatican representative!" snapped the Cardinal. "If you are not up to it, send an envoy."

With that the Cardinal continued on with other matters while Alessandro sat back in his chair and sighed, this time with relief.

The envoy sent from Rome arrived safely, as would have any travelling cardinal. The emblems from the Vatican were enough to let any man know that he was not one to be trifled with. The envoy sat upon his horse looking at the church and sneered, before dismounting and tying his ride to the palings we had erected for such. Then he made way inside.

We were in the midst of communion and the envoy took his place within the last pew and watched intently. The man may have been sent as a scout for Rome but this did not diminish the fact that he was a devout follower of the church as ascribed by the papacy. He took in every detail, from the simple cup that held the wine through to the way I was dressed - still within the brown robe which I now wore with pride, symbolising my humility and all that I had shed in order to serve our Lord.

The envoy had expected a lunatic. He had also expected to be witness to some ritual which verged upon the ancient ways that had been so hard fought to eradicate. Instead he felt that he was being shown something entirely different. As he watched me he felt a calm wash through his body. The agitation at arriving during a mass and the frustration at having to wait dissipated and he closed his eyes to begin some prayer. He then felt a gentle hand upon his shoulder. It was Sabatino standing beside him.

"Communion is almost complete. Do you care to partake?" Sabatino invited.

The envoy stood and walked to the altar where I was waiting. I looked into his eyes and realised he was new to the congregation which made me smile. It was not until I had placed the morsel of bread into his mouth that I happened to see the emblem of the Vatican upon his vest and my smile grew even larger. He returned to his pew and I finished the prayers and the service.

He stayed in the pew as all others left and I remained upon the altar knowing that he was waiting to speak to me. As the last person walked out the door I went to him.

"You have travelled some way," I began to which he nodded in agreement.

"I come from the Vatican. We have received word as to your—practices here and I was sent to report on what it is that you are doing," he stated directly trying as hard as he could to remain authoritative and strong.

"And tell me, what do you see?" I asked.

The envoy opened his mouth to speak but his voice faltered and no words came from him. Instead he looked past me at the altar and then dropped his head.

When he returned to Rome his conversation with the cardinal was simple and concise.

"He preaches in peace and integrity," he reported as Cardinal Alessandro raised an eyebrow.

"And how did you come to this conclusion?" Alessandro asked.

"I did not feel like leaving," was the only answer the envoy could muster.

The visit from the Vatican raised something within me. I decided that it was time for a pilgrimage to Rome, with the possibility of an audience with Pope Innocent III. I knew this might be fanciful but my growing ministry would make me something of concern to the Pope. Such was the interest in my teaching that I would now travel to nearby villages to preach and I was also taking more men into my brotherhood to support this as well as learn my ways.

This in itself was a blessing so that when I did finally decide to travel to Rome, I could appoint Bernardo, a local Assisi man who had joined my church, to oversee teaching in my absence. Sabatino and Morico were more than happy to accompany me.

"I shall send for money from my father," offered Sabatino.

"Sabatino, do you think our Lord worried about money as he made way to teach and know people?" I asked.

Sabatino smiled. "I have no doubt that money was the least of his concerns."

So we set upon the road to Rome with a simple satchel of bread and cheese. We had no idea of where we would sleep at night or where our meals would come from. Instead we had our faith and trust to provide for us, which they did in plenty.

We would stop at a well or fountain to fill our skins with water and a conversation would begin with a local.

"Who are you?" "Where are you from?" "Where are you going?" "What business do you have upon the road?" These were the stock questions that people would use to engage with us, often as they warily measured my simple robe as well as the lack of horses and goods that we carried with us.

We relished these points of contact with others as we walked. They gave us opportunity to share who we were, and then inevitably what we were teaching. Each conversation and the reactions we evoked only confirmed to me that people were hungry for the truth of Christ's teaching. They were aching to know God without the pomp and complexity that the Church now represented to them.

Many times a simple interaction would lead to an invitation to speak to a gathering. This in turn would result in a meal and accommodation from someone in attendance.

We spoke the truth of the Lord and in turn he provided for us; protecting and nurturing us as we made way to Rome, so that in the ten days of our travelling we not once went hungry or slept in the open. Every day our faith and trust was proven true and our dedication and commitment to our purpose was renewed. We arrived in Rome even more determined than when we had left Assisi. Rome on the other hand provided us with new opportunities that at first seemed far from encouraging.

As we approached the outskirts of our fabled and lauded city, you could feel its energy reach out to grab you and pull you into its web. I even heard Sabatino grunt as we saw its buildings appear before us and the noise of its population began to reach our ears.

"Urgh! I hate cities! Give me a quiet village any day," he muttered.

I turned to look at him and saw his shoulders were slouched and his brow was creased.

"Sabatino, you look like someone I have not seen before," I said.

Sabatino turned to me and his brow furrowed even more. "I always feel this way near a city, so I guess this is how I look when I am near or in a city," he said and shrugged his shoulders.

I thought about how I had felt as I had walked back into Assisi to face the magistrate and my father. How those voices and those feelings inside me, the ones that I had let go of, returned to me as I walked back into the town.

"Sabatino, we cannot let a place or a person diminish or change us. Do you want to be this person here in Rome? Or do you want to be the man who chose to teach with me?" I asked him.

He looked at me somewhat puzzled. "I don't understand."

"Do you want to walk your truth - God's truth - in each moment or are you willing to be distracted by a place or a person?"

Sabatino looked down and I could tell his mind was wrestling with this notion. Then he took a deep breath and looked up. As he squared his shoulders he declared, "Nothing is more important than the work we have to do!"

With that we now walked into Rome completely assured of who we were and what we were doing.

I will never forget what it felt like to stand before Saint Peter's church. This was nothing like the palatial building that stands there now. In my time it was a much simpler affair, the first of its three incarnations. Emperor Constantine, a true visionary, had claimed our Christian holy sites and built monuments to herald their significance. In Jerusalem a church rose over the site of the crucifixion and tomb of our Lord and Saviour. Here in Rome he had taken Nero's Circus, the site of hundreds of Christian martyrdoms, most notably the noble apostle Peter, and tore it down. In its place now stood a grand cathedral.

It was so beautiful how Constantine had taken a place of so much hatred and torment and transformed it into a place of reflection. The three of us stood and looked over the place where our Christian forefathers and mothers had been beaten, mocked and crucified. Each one of us took to prayer. We asked that God never forget the honour they gave to his name. Then we asked of their spirits to guide and support us in our work.

We walked slowly into the church and made way to the altar. There was a steady stream of pilgrims ahead of us. We waited patiently for them to make their way ahead of us. Many spoke gentle quiet prayers, some stepped in silence. I heard different languages, saw varied coloured skins and clothing, yet we were all there with the same love and devotion. I was overcome by the beauty of the unity between us all so that when I arrived at the altar my tears flowed freely down my cheeks.

Sabatino, Morico and I kneeled before the altar and realised the truth of our pilgrimage. We may have travelled to gain an audience with the Pope but the truth of Rome was buried beneath this altar. The body of Saint Peter, the most significant of Jesus' male followers lay here.

After his torture and crucifixion by Nero for his own amusement, Peter's body had been buried here, along with other martyrs. Constantine in his wisdom ensured Peter's internment would be preserved forever by designing the church so the altar, the place of communion and the speaking of the gospel, would be over him for eternity.

Jesus had asked of Peter to be the rock upon which his teaching would be founded and Constantine had made sure this had become something more literal. As I knelt there in my brief moment to do so, I contemplated this. I imagined Peter was still with us, standing at the altar ready to speak.

I could picture him smiling down upon me and my companions. Not because we had made pilgrimage to his remains but because we were now continuing on the legacy of the apostles. I took a deep breath and understood even more of what my calling to the Lord was set to do for humanity.

My reverie was short-lived though as a young priest asked us to move along.

"I am sorry, but there are so many wanting to pray with Saint Peter," he said.

We all nodded and made way to the side of the church to make our exit. Outside we walked in silence for some time, not even sure where we should be headed. Finally Morico stopped and asked, "Where are we going now?"

My first impulse was to answer "Everywhere!" but I simply smiled and said, "let's make way to Saint John's and see if the Pope will receive us."

CHAPTER ELEVEN

The basilica of Saint John was not so far from that of Saint Peter's, and it was there that the Pope resided when in Rome. The Vatican as it is known now was still generations away from being built. When we arrived at the church it was surrounded by beggars, but then Rome was full of beggars. As with most cities it provided the best chance of receiving alms or some scrap of food from the large population. However Rome had even more opportunities for those in need.

Rome was full of Christians and the Christian tradition was filled with teachings of compassion and charity. The very life of Jesus was that of treating the less advantaged with the respect and dignity that any of God's children were worthy of. So many pilgrims saw the beggars as their chance to pay service to Jesus' work by handing out food and money, offering healing prayers and for the very rare beggar there might be the opportunity to be hired as a servant.

It was like an industry unto itself and indelibly linked to the church. We had walked amongst them almost invisible. Morico and Sabatino were now also dressed in the simple brown robe I had adopted so that for the most part we were mistaken for the needy. It was only when someone could see that we were well fed and healthy that we were deemed otherwise.

"Why do you dress like that?" a priest at Saint Peter's had asked of us.

"Because we have no need to dress otherwise," was my reply.

The look he gave us was replicated on the face of the priest who opened a small window within the door at Saint John's to answer our knock.

"Alms are given on Sunday!" he snapped and pointed to a notice nailed to the left of the door.

"We are not here for alms. We are here to ask for audience with His Holiness. I am Francis, a brother of Christ who preaches the gospel in Assisi," I explained.

Once more he looked me over and then to the men beside me. I saw in his eyes that he knew exactly who I was. My name had been mentioned many times within these walls.

"Wait here," he said and then slammed closed the opening.

He returned ten minutes later. Enough time so that I knew an honest effort had been made to pass on my request but short enough to let me know that I would not be received.

"You shall have no audience," he said and quickly shut the opening before we could ask why.

To be honest I was not interested in explanations and this snub did not affect me in any way. I turned and nodded to Sabatino and Morico.

"That is disappointing," muttered Morico.

"We do not need recognition from anyone to teach our Lord's work. And our Lord will not see us any differently because of this man's choice," I said and they both smiled in agreement.

I looked past them and into the square we would make way through. It was now mid afternoon and it was filled with beggars and the ill, all hoping that being close to the church and His Holiness would present them with some respite from their suffering.

I watched as some wealthy pilgrims walked through the crowd brushing off the hands as they made way to the church. I did not judge them. There is only so much food or money one can hand out. Instead I imagined what it must be like to not know when you would be handed something. What was it like to be ignored? What did it feel like when someone did grant you their charity?

You would live each day with only faith to truly sustain you, no matter what meals you were provided and no matter what clothes were upon you. These beggars here in Rome lived with the absolute trust that they would be supported by the energies of Christ and those who followed him.

Standing here now, in my robes, with only a day's food within my satchel I realised I was not so unalike. However the differences were vast when you looked beyond the clothing and sustenance. I had a home to return to in my church at Assisi. My devotion to teaching Christ's words provided for me, even as I travelled.

I recalled being back in my prison cell. Even that had the comfort of being sheltered and a regular meal. This was something else entirely. This was being taken back to the essence of survival and something inside me wanted to know this experience.

"We have nowhere yet to stay tonight do we?" I asked.

"No, but there is a lodge that receives male pilgrims in return for chores," Sabatino offered.

"My brothers, you are free to make your way there," I smiled. "I shall stay here in the square tonight."

"Francis, no!" Sabatino said resisting the urge to raise his voice. "These people are desperate. You do not want to put yourself at their mercy, especially when the dark will hide their actions. Beside you will be sleeping amongst a myriad of diseases that the night air will invite into your body!"

"And do you suppose the Lord would abandon me just because the sun has gone down?" I asked.

Sabatino sighed and I continued on. "I want this experience. If we are to serve all men and humanity then I want to know the depths as well as the glory of this life. Did not Christ walk with the lepers and the destitute to share his word so that their souls too would know redemption? If all are worthy of the Lord's words then so is their life worthy of my experience. This will be my chance to know humility. True humility. We have all led privileged lives. We live now in simplicity but not in the humility that these people do."

I am not so sure that either truly understood the magnitude of what I was hoping to convey but it hardly mattered.

"I won't leave you here," piped up Morico. "I won't be able to sleep from worrying about you. I may as well not sleep whilst out here on the cobbles."

I looked to Sabatino who simply nodded in agreement.

Even though their concerns were of being in the square at night, we had many hours of daylight before us. I walked about watching those upon their knees with their hands out. They did not look up, but just held their palms upwards ready to receive. Something about this called to my essence. I found a place on the cobbles and lowered myself.

I pulled the hood of my robe forward so that as I lowered my head my face would be hidden. There would be no eye contact or looks of pleading to draw upon sympathies. Then I raised my hands up level with my shoulders, my palms open and ready.

The first few minutes felt like an eternity. My arms began to ache. I heard my mind asking question after question. Should I lower my hood? Should I be calling out for mercy as many did? Should I walk and approach pilgrims or the local nobility? I took a deep breath and felt that beautiful presence of the Holy Spirit fill me.

It was the same as when it had happened in my prison cell and I realised this place was no different. The routine of begging was relentless and mundane. It was cold and damp at times and those who seemed to provide anything for you also treated you with disdain.

The first coin I received was thrown at me so that it bounced out of my hand and was quickly grabbed by another beggar nearby. I hardly noticed him wrap his fist tightly around it and run away. Instead I was looking to my benefactor. All I saw was a swish of his bright robes as he continued onwards. His servant following close behind flicked his hand at me, signalling to look away as though my eyes were not worthy to look upon this donor.

This made me smile at the irony. The man wanted the glory of giving, but no association with the recipient of his charity. It was how religion was now. Take Jesus' teaching but have no connection to its truth. To sit within your church for the social approval but not live its teachings once you were out the doors. It was no wonder that those who were now responsible for sharing the Lord's wisdom were also so detached.

I imagined this Middle Eastern man making his way into the church of Saint John kneeling and saying his prayers. He would return home and in his village he would be revered for making way to a holy site. He would speak of the wondrous buildings, and the honour of walking the places that the disciples did. Then he would speak of the poverty and how he had given as his act of compassion.

Yet he did not even know what my face looked like. He did not know my story or why I was seemingly destitute or that his coin had not even made its way to my purse. All he knew was his action and what this would achieve for his standing with what he believed God to be.

He was merely a product of what he and so many others had been taught as to what was an acceptable form of Christianity. There were others who had their servants hand out the food and alms, in the fear they may contract an illness or simply from the repulsion of interacting with such low standing beings.

Each time I felt an offering land upon my palms I would look up to see if I could somehow make a connection to the benefactor. This was part curiosity to see who they were, but mostly I just wanted them to see my face and to acknowledge that I was a person. Using my hood to hide my face had been a wonderful inspiration as it actually made many of them feel more comfortable to give to me. It was a technique that many beggars adopted. For many it helped them show their piety and humility. To the donors it made giving much easier. Not all those who gave were so disconnected. There were those who would stop and offer a prayer but they were few and far between.

Much has been made of my time begging as this led to when I took my vow of poverty. It was said that this activity was about denouncing luxuries and this was true. When the three of us finished living like this for five days we were different men. It was not so much from having lived without the comforts we had known in our family homes or even without the security of our parish to provide for us as we had all been living simply for over a year now. This experience with the beggars had shown us another depth to impoverishment.

It was not that of living in desperation or with the constant risk of death looming over them. The beggars knew that God would provide for them, and for some death was a welcome respite from the harshness of their life. Our vow of poverty was about making an oath to never have possessions or wealth distract us from the truth of the Lord's words. Even more than that, it was our commitment to never let such things disconnect us from any of God's children no matter their circumstance.

As I knelt in that square, no richer or poorer than when I left Assisi, I felt the equality of all that God had created. I felt that I was no better than any man or woman who begged beside me. I felt that I was no lesser than anyone who gave to me regardless of their intentions or altruism. Each one of us walked this Earth with a life gifted by God. It was our human foibles that made us classify, judge and segregate, and the greatest of these follies was wealth.

I recalled the tale of Jesus overturning the tables of the moneylenders at the temple and I knew the depths of his passion and anger as he did this. He too in that moment had renounced this aspect of our human condition. It had been something ingrained for thousands of years, that money makes us superior people or deserving of more privilege when in fact it did neither.

No one actively chooses poverty. It seems something that fate belies them. I knew that in making a conscious choice to live this way, I would not only set my internal energies and keep my connection to God pure but I would also make this another aspect of my teaching.

I had seen how wealth had stripped my father of warmth and closeness to his family. Possessions and social standing had become his reason for existence, yet inside he was hollow and removed from the joys of life.

As I knelt in that square I realised the gift I had given myself in rejecting the wealth I had been born into and was entitled to. It had begun in my prison cell, when stripped of all comforts I had nothing but what I felt inside of me; that internal energy that we call our soul, that is our innate and continual connection to God, that feeds our connection to life. I had my external distractions torn away and this had allowed me to go within to a purity that so few people know.

I felt it again as I begged. There was nothing of me that was absent as I knelt before the world with no possessions or adornments. All that I needed to know of was what I held inside of me and each time I felt this and allowed its presence into my experience then it grew and I loved it even more.

The less there was outside of me, then the more I knew my soul.

The more I knew my soul, the more I knew God and could work to comprehend the essence of his teaching. Nothing would make me more joyful than to share this with the world so that they too would know of their birthright to live in God's love with their own unique connection.

That is why I took my vow of poverty. That is why each man or woman who chose to teach alongside me would also be asked to do this. To touch the grandeur of our creator, we had to know the simplicity of being human.

I returned to Assisi from my pilgrimage with renewed vigour, passion and commitment. This in itself was enough to attract more worshippers before I spoke any words. It is wonderful how when you choose to fill your life with God's love and your connection to your own spirit how it then radiates out to others.

My humble church was filled to capacity for every service and sometimes in-between as people chose to sit and pray there. I travelled to nearby villages and preached in homes or open fields, wherever I could to share the teachings of Our Lord and Saviour. Nothing warmed my heart more than to not just have people around me, but to look into their eyes and see that they were taking the words into their hearts.

I had people come to me afterwards to offer meals or accommodation. Some handed me baskets of fresh produce, baked goods and skins of wine. I would keep what would serve me and share the excess with the needy as they crossed my path. The greatest gift that any of them would ever offer me though was to see them smile as they would share how long it had been since they had wanted to go to church or hear a sermon. They would thank me for bringing them back to God's word and that was all I could ever hope my teaching would do.

Young men would approach me and ask to teach with me and while this was most flattering I also knew it was necessity. The desire to hear my style of sharing was outgrowing my human capabilities to do so. I soon had a small brotherhood to assist me and also offer mass and communion in my stead. Each one was received with the love and honour that I was, and I know this was because it was the word of God spoken with integrity that people were craving and not my presence.

Even more than the requirement of physical support I too knew this brotherhood was part of my promise to rebuild the church as God had asked of me. I had restyled the way people were hearing the gospel. I had broken the barriers of who was welcomed and how, but thus far we were doing so within a small area. I knew this brotherhood was going to be key to showing reform in a far greater way that would truly change the Christian model as it was now.

However I also had patience in how this would unfold. This was born of my infinite trust in my connection to God. It had not failed me once, not even when the Pope had refused me audience in Rome. I knew that was merely a test and even more so I knew that it was God's sign that I needed to do more work as my experience begging had shown me.

This was a huge part of my energy when I returned to Assisi. When people asked whether I was disappointed that the Pope had not received me I would shake my head and smile.

"Through him God has given us time to work even harder and more graciously, so that when he does we will be even grander and our achievements will have more merit!" I would answer.

I believed and accepted this with every fibre of my being. This was what I also felt drew more people to us and what gathered my acolytes. I did not return to Assisi as a shunned man, I stood before them as someone who had dared to ask of the Pope and returned more determined to show my worthiness. That in itself was inspiring and showed hope to those around me.

✸ CHAPTER TWELVE

Much has been said of my love and honour of animals. That I am the patron saint of animals fills my soul with gratitude. I am eternally awed at having this granted to my memory.

The animal world taught me much and that in turn shaped me as a teacher. I did not have any supernatural ability to communicate with them. Much as I believed every person could have their own connection and communication with God, I too believed that they could commune with animals. These abilities are not gifts or talents; they are inherent within us all. The key is in allowing it.

The nest within my first church showed me much. That day when I looked up at the small bird sitting by her home, her babies tucked safely within the twigs and straw, began a whole new dimension of my life. I knew that in having compassion and respect for animals then it would somehow show people that there should be no bounds within our human world.

It was so simple that it took a while for people to understand.

"Let me clear that nest for you. Or you will soon be overrun," offered one of the local men who came to worship.

I gently placed my hand upon his shoulder. "They are God's creatures, as are you and I, and I will never deny them their place within the church just as I would never to any man, woman or child."

The man nodded but I could still feel his hesitancy. He lifted one eyebrow and smiled. "So can I bring my goat along tomorrow?"

I know it was in jest and in no way from any meanness but something inside me stirred. What if tomorrow my church was filled with animals all seeking their connection with God, their creator?

Now a sensible man would have dismissed the thought as ridiculous and infantile. I, however, carried that thought to my bed where I lay looking to the shadows above me and pondering it over and over.

Perhaps a calf could not ever know of the words of the gospel, but surely it could feel the love of God and sense its purpose in a more enriched way. Perhaps the animal's owner could stand by them and hear the teachings then return home with a new respect for their animals. Most importantly, they would all carry home the blessings of a God that created them in love and honour. That surely would have to touch their lives in some way.

Thus what would have seemed an incredulous idea became something of worth and depth. I announced it and sent my priests to spread the word.

"Bring your animals to be blessed," was how it was announced.

"There is no way this can be held within the church," said Sabatino. "Besides, the mess and smell would be horrendous."

Though I had no worries about my church smelling like a barn we did indeed hold the mass outdoors. It was simple logic that was confirmed when people arrived with cows and horses.

The noises and smells were glorious as they gathered and to look out and see not just my usual mix of people, but now the variety of animals as well made my heart swell. So much so that my voice nearly faltered as I began.

I stopped and took a breath to gather myself and in that moment the warmth of the Holy Spirit surged though me. I closed my eyes and raised my hands with open palms facing out to the congregation. As I did I felt the energy of spirit course through me and out to each and every person and animal gathered.

I opened my eyes and looked upon them. My body tingled with what had just happened and I knew that no words would ever explain or do this justice, but the warmth within me that remained reminded me that what I would speak would be blessed and perfect.

"Let us give thanks to our creator. Dear God in Heaven above, we give thanks for all you have created in your image that we can gather here today..."

And thus began my first service for animals.

Later that day I went into the church and was tidying around the altar in preparation for our evening prayers. I was smoothing a cloth over its wooden surface when I heard a flutter by my right ear. My little bird, the one who had allowed us into her home to reclaim this derelict building for God, landed just before my right hand.

I stayed as still as could be as she looked me up and down intently then let her eyes meet mine. She turned her head from side to side and it was as though she was talking with me. I remained still and smiled. I did not speak but I thanked her for what she had shown me and what that had allowed.

My little friend raised herself up and spread out her wings then sang a sweet, short song to me. In that song she agreed and thanked me for blessing her.

Our masses for the blessed creatures became a regular event, held

74

once a month and they grew such that several of my brothers would travel to hold them in nearby villages as well. It was no surprise that within a short time I soon looked out and saw that one of the men holding the lead of his horse wore the emblem of the Pope upon his tunic.

I simply nodded and smiled. This was my sign to return to Rome. I knew now that the Pope would receive me.

I chose the first eleven brothers who had joined the order to travel alongside me to Rome. It seemed fitting that just as Jesus had travelled with his disciples as a band of brothers to teach then so should my brotherhood. They were not my assistants or any lesser than I. Each man was as committed and connected to God's word as I was. They would not have been by my side otherwise.

"It is a shame that we have not another man so we would truly replicate the Lord and his twelve apostles," said Bernardo.

"We are twelve instead of thirteen as there is no Judas amongst you," I replied and looked at each one of them. "This is perfect as is. I know with all my heart that you join me with complete dedication to all I began and that nothing will distract or compromise that commitment you have, not just as priests but as teachers."

They all nodded in agreement.

We made way to Rome easily. The larger group of us now gathered more attention and more opportunity to share. As we walked we sang and clapped our hands to create music, so that there were times when people would simply join us to become part of a song. We travelled in joy to spread the word of the Lord with love and that in itself restored faith in people who crossed our path.

As I saw Rome's buildings ahead I turned to Sabatino and upon his face was a broad smile and not one shred of the disdain that had been there when we last approached. This smile was upon the faces of all the men around me.

"No matter what happens within this city, we remain men of God and his gospel. Walk with pride and carry his love with every step," I said but the words were hardly necessary.

We went directly to the same door at the side of Saint John's but there was no answer. I waited for an hour and then sent the men onto the lodges that received pilgrims while Sabatino and I waited for several more hours in the hope that our knocking would eventually be answered.

"They are ignoring us," sighed Sabatino.

"Yes they are, my brother," I replied. "Perhaps we should be kind to our hands and stop knocking today."

In my heart I knew we would make it through that door somehow and I had the patience to continue as I knew my brothers did too. I did not anticipate that this would continue on for two more days.

While Sabatino and I would stand at the door, knocking intermittently, the others would walk the square praying with the beggars, tending to small wounds or ailments and sharing food. I looked at them dressed in the simple long brown hooded tunic that I wore. They blended in with the beggars as though they were always here. I even saw one of them shoved by a pilgrim as he needed to pass to make way to the cathedral.

That act did make me angry but more importantly it reminded me of why our order was so important. It reminded me of God's request to rebuild his church. I turned and knocked the hardest I ever had upon that door now and called out.

"I am Francis of Assisi! I request audience with His Holiness in the name of Our Father the Almighty, in the name of our Saviour Jesus of Nazareth and in the name of the Holy Spirit!"

It was as much of a prayer as it was a demand, yet still nothing stirred behind the wooden door.

"Let us rest," suggested Sabatino and I nodded.

We walked to the opposite side of the square, gathering the rest of our group as we did so. There we sat quietly and looked back upon the cathedral and the scene before us. More pilgrims and priests wove amongst the beggars.

Bernardo raised his hand and pointed to two of the priests dressed in elaborate robes that showed they were something significant.

"Isn't that Bishop Guido from Assisi?" he said.

We all focussed our eyes where he pointed and in an instant I knew it was. With that I began to walk quickly back through the square with my men behind me. I realised that I would not make it to the Bishop before he disappeared within the cathedral. I quickened my pace so now I was running as were my brothers. They knew as well as I did that Guido was our opportunity to be heard.

As we got closer we all slowed our pace so that when I finally stepped in front of the Bishop and his companion we appeared composed.

"Bishop Guido, how nice to see you," I said and bowed to show some form of respect.

"Oh yes Francis. I heard you were making pilgrimage," he said and though he did not grimace I felt his discomfort anyway.

Bishop Guido had hoped we would not cross paths. We had developed what you might call an uneasy alliance back in Assisi. He could not question or denounce me as that would have given me even more attention and then possibly lost him even more worshippers. I knew this, thus kept away from his cathedral and not once did I speak ill of his priests or how they conducted themselves. It was a wonderful balance that served us both.

"I imagine you are here to speak the concerns of our parish?" I asked.

Guido sighed. "But of course Francis... as well as to partake my own pilgrimage. Every visit to Rome brings us closer to our Lord."

I smiled with a clenched jaw defying every instinct to argue that it was our souls that connected us to God and not some location, but I knew I had much more important matters to achieve with this conversation.

"Yes indeed Bishop. Perhaps I could ask of you as our parish representative here, that when you speak with His Holiness that you suggest he may receive our brotherhood?"

"And for what purpose?" The Bishop raised his eyebrow and I knew I had touched a deep fear within him. Instantly he saw me asking for our ordination so that we would have the right to preach in the main cathedral of Assisi.

I took a deep breath. "Bishop, we have no designs upon your power. We want to be recognised so that we can take our teachings further afield with the validation of the church. I will not see my brothers imprisoned for heresy when all we want to do is share the love and joy of the Lord's word."

Guido sighed and looked to the man beside him as though to offer him apology for my interruption to their journey. This was the first time that I looked upon the man as well and I saw that he was dressed in the robes of a cardinal.

He looked at me and smiled and I returned the gesture with a small bow to show my respect.

"Hello Cardinal, I am Francis of Assisi."

"I know who you are," he interrupted. "I doubt there is a priest in Rome who has not heard of you and what you do." He looked to the men around me. "You have gathered a noble order as well."

While the bishop and I had spoken the cardinal had measured me closely, as well as the men around me. He didn't just take in how we were dressed, or how many of us there were. The Cardinal looked at how we stood, the expressions on our faces and the sense of my words. This was a man who saw more than with his eyes and heard more than with his ears.

I may have thought Guido was our blessing from God to get us beyond that door into the residence behind Saint John's, but he was merely the gift that would see me meet this man; Cardinal-Bishop Giovanni di Paolo of Sabina. The Cardinal was not just one of the men who worked closely with the Pope; he was the Pope's confessor. In the Catholic Church there was no one who knew His Holiness better than the man who heard his deepest fears, weaknesses and faults.

That this man now stood before me and saw my truth was the blessing that we had been praying for. The Cardinal had heard of all we had been doing and had been following any updates with amused interest. There had been something about me that had intrigued him and now as I stood before him, he saw it clearly.

I reminded the Cardinal of himself at the age I now was, when he was fresh in the priesthood, full of ideals and brimming with passion. Not that the Cardinal had lost any of his passion for serving his Lord, it was just that now it was somewhat buried under the weight of his position and what this expected of him. As he looked at me though, he felt something of his youthful self return.

"I will speak of you to the Pope," he said with a smile. "But know this is a man with many demands upon him; both holy and human! I trust there will be no tantrums nor loss of devotion should you be refused?"

I smiled and shook my head. "We were refused once before and lost nothing of our desire or commitment."

As they walked away Bishop Guido seethed and the Cardinal could feel the heat off his face.

"Bishop, if you live in fear of losing your position then you shall. Have you no trust in your place with God?" said the Cardinal.

Guido muttered a reply and the Cardinal, though he did not hear it, knew it was merely a cursory and expected response to end the dialogue. The Cardinal in his wisdom left the discussion at that.

It was a simple conversation held with the Pope. One does not allow another man to take his confession without having respect or consideration for his opinion or counsel.

"We have all heard much of his work. Would it not be beneficial to give him audience? That way he will be encouraged to remain within the fold rather than create heresy or show rebellion to you?"

Pope Innocent III nodded slowly.

"I will see them tomorrow."

A young acolyte was sent to find us and pass on the message. We didn't realise who he was at first. He just looked lost, ducking through the crowd on the square, peering at faces. Then he began to call out.

"Francis! Francis of Assisi! Is there anyone here of his order?"

We started to laugh and then Elias called out to him.

"Right here!"

The young man walked over and looked at us all quizzically.

"You're the monks from Assisi?" he asked as he scanned us up and down.

"Yes. I am Francis," I smiled.

He shrugged his shoulders then squared them, placed his feet against each other and cupped his hands within one another. Then he cleared his throat, tilted his chin up and spoke as formally as he could.

"His Holiness Pope Innocent the Third has received your request for audience. His Holiness accepts this request and has approved your presence at the papal residence tomorrow morning. Please arrive at the ringing of the tenth hour bells."

He finished and bowed, so we all did in return. He turned and began to walk away, then stopped and spun around, throwing his hands in the air.

"Oh I forgot to ask! Do you accept?" he said as he screwed up his face.

"Oh we accept!" I replied.

We waited until he was out of earshot before we allowed ourselves to laugh; partly at the comedy of our invitation but mostly from the joy of finally getting to meet the Pope and speak our worth.

The next morning we arrived in the square before Saint John's well before the bells rang for the tenth hour. There would be no chance that we would be late and then have our opportunity revoked. We were all calm and clear, even though there were nerves of excitement.

The night before we had sat and discussed what would occur.

"Make no mistake my brothers, we will be tested on our faith and our knowledge, but I know that I can look at each one of you and have absolute faith in whatever you will say. If you feel your words failing, call to the Holy Spirit to fill you and let them flow. If you are not speaking, listen to what is being said with your utmost focus and devotion. There will be much around us to distract and waiver our attention. Make every breath, thought and word about the dedication you have to restoring the church's connection to the truth of our Saviour and the Lord's word," I had said strongly to them.

Then we prayed together. We prayed that the Lord would show the Pope our sincerity and integrity. We prayed for the Holy Spirit to fill us with its wisdom and guidance. We prayed that we would accept whatever outcome presented itself at the meeting's completion.

The next morning we woke, bathed and ate a light breakfast. Then we took to prayer again. When we heard the bells for the ninth hour we began our journey to Saint John's.

We walked with such determination and assuredness that people cleared the way for us. Not one obstacle arose before us and I heard God speak to me so clearly:

"Walk in your majesty as a beacon of my love and nothing will stand in your way."

In that moment I knew this meeting would be fortuitous and when I shared this with my brothers as we stood before Saint John's I know that any nerves which may have lingered were erased.

We gathered before that dreaded door once more and before I could even knock, the small shutter within it swung open and a stern face looked out upon us.

"Stand so I can count you. I am not to allow any more than twelve in. I was told there were twelve of you. Move so I can see how many there are!" he snapped.

Each of us moved so he could get a clear view.

"I have a guard here, so if you have any ideas of someone else sneaking in to join you, it won't happen!"

"I assure you that my entire entourage is here present. There will be no others attempting to join us," I said calmly.

He grunted and shut the window. Then we heard locks sliding and bars moving and finally the door swung open.

"Quick! Quick! Quick before the beggars see the door open and mob to it. One time I could not even shut the door," he said motioning with his hand to beckon us in.

Once we were all in he closed the door and went through the process of sliding bars and locks back into place. We were now standing in a fairly nondescript hallway lined with just enough candles to provide ease of walking. We also noted there was no guard and understood the priest's urgency not just in checking our numbers but that we entered quickly.

Now complete with having reinstated the security of the door, he pushed past us to lead the way.

"You are early but I should say that will bode well with His Excellency. He is not one to tolerate lack of respect especially to logistical matters. That is part of why he was chosen to lead the church. Faith does not necessarily translate well into administrative abilities. You might want to remember that should you have aspirations to join us here in Rome," he blathered.

I heard a few of the men stifle laughs and turned to shake my head. Now was not the time to lose our composure no matter the unintentional entertainment.

The hallway turned to the left and I imagined we were now behind the main body of the church. The altar and holy sacrament would not be so far from where we were and I made the sign of the cross to acknowledge it. The priest caught this and looked at me with open consternation.

"I imagine we are close by the blessed host are we not?" I offered and he nodded.

"But heavens, if I did that every time I passed something holy here my hand would never rest!" he responded.

Now I could not help but laugh and the priest joined me.

We were taken to a large room, lined with paintings and tapestries. It was ornate but not to the point of being garish. A large chair sat to the middle of the wall facing the huge doors that opened into the room. Beside it were smaller but similarly elaborate chairs. Everything spoke of wealth but not opulence.

"Step aside for His Holiness."

It was the Cardinal of Sabina leading the way into the room for the Pope. His Holiness followed behind him and then several other cardinals and bishops. We parted like the Red Sea did for Moses, expecting the Pope to simply walk through us and take his seat. Instead he stopped as he stepped into the room, looked upon us and smiled.

Then he took each man's hand in his own and looked into their eyes, so that every one of our group had their personal moment with him. It was humbling and overwhelming to be embraced this way. It was also His Holiness' way of feeling what each man was like and how each of us took this honour made my heart sing.

Each man looked straight back into the Pope's eyes before bowing their head in reverence. Each one showed conviction and strength, yet respect and reverence. I knew that by the time he was standing before me most of our work had been achieved.

"I am Francis," I said as much as a pronouncement as it was an introduction.

His Holiness nodded and smiled as he held my hand. "Yes. We

have much to talk about," he said simply and then made way to his chair.

I was invited to speak my case but it did not feel like I had anything to prove. With or without this man's approval I would still live and teach about our connection to God. However I also knew that God's will to have this taught in a new way would need this church's support. Assisi and her neighbouring towns may have embraced us, but to send out men to teach elsewhere would need much more.

The Pope listened politely with a face that remained expressionless, trained from years of receiving confessions and petitions much like mine. When I was finished he nodded but still did not either smile or frown.

"Are you aware of how many men come to me to ask for validation and approval each year?" he asked me.

"No, Your Holiness, but I imagine it is many," I replied.

Now he smiled. "You know how to answer without commitment. You would make a good politician or lawyer."

I drew a quick breath. This was intended to cut me and I knew his comment was a test in itself. As I realised this I slowed my breath and smiled.

"Your Holiness, I am aware of the heretics who wish to pull the church apart to satisfy the delusions of their mind and the rewards they believe it will bestow upon them. I can imagine how many come here to challenge you, or hope you will embrace them and change centuries of reform to suit their agendas. Please know this is far from why we stand before you. We have a desire within ourselves to know the purity of a relationship with God and we have a passion to share this with others. I know we are doing things differently but our essence is the same. We have brought people back to God and his words, many of whom had long grown tired or confused by how it was being shared. We have given them back the soul of Jesus and the redemption through him which was offered to us. We have no desire to usurp or destroy. We simply wish to bring God's children back to his love and safety. To let them know that the joy of life is not to struggle or pay tithe but to know that all is well in God's love and to return this to him with the same love and honour. We live simply to show people that their connection to the Holy Spirit is simple and—and—Your Holiness they are embracing this! It is our passion to let so many more know this."

I finished and the Pope's face finally changed. He seemed to slump back into his chair and I saw the Cardinal turn to look at him as though he too wanted to measure his reaction.

Then the Pope leaned forward and put his hand out.

"Come," he said.

I stepped forward and took his hand. Then I knelt down and looked up to his face. He placed his other hand on my forehead and lowered his head in prayer. I too lowered my head to join him. We said no words aloud but I know he was asking for God's direction and advice. I prayed that God would show him the truth of my words.

He pulled his hands away.

"Stand up," he said simply.

I did and once more we looked each other in the eye.

"You have board for the night?" he asked and I nodded. "Return tomorrow and I will share my final response with you."

"Thank you," was all I could manage to say in reply.

We were once more escorted back to the door that would open into the square. All of us walked in silence, still somewhat in awe of what we had achieved in just being in the presence of our church's leader, let alone to have spoken our cause. Within that silence though so much more was going on within me and within my men.

As each of us walked, we stood just a little bit taller, our stride was just a little more graceful and our breath was just a little bit slower. Within each and every one of us the warmth of the Holy Spirit was coursing its love through our veins and not one of us was absent of its presence. It was deeper than that of course. It was not just the blessing of Our Lord to grant us the confidence to return to request the Pope's validation. It was our own spirit rejoicing our strength in declaring our love for our work and even more, our soul connection to God.

We filed out through the door, nodding our thanks to the custodian priest who had been our escort and host. Then we all walked into the church of Saint John's and prayed. We thanked God for the blessing of the Pope's willingness to receive us. We prayed to the Holy Mother Mary for the compassion to accept his decision. We prayed to Jesus that we would be as honourable a teacher as he was.

This we did for several hours, until our bodies cried out for rest and sustenance. Then we made way to our lodge for the night.

As we ate our soup and bread, we talked gently of the revelations and feelings we had received while praying.

"I saw our church in the hills of Assisi but it was much grander and a great beam of light came from the heavens and lit it up," said Morico.

"I saw us walking the streets of the Holy Land just as Jesus did," said Giovanni.

I smiled and nodded as each one spoke then they looked to me hoping I had some insights to share.

"I heard no words, nor did I see any images. I felt the strength of our spirits united to share what we believe, and I know this will be rewarded. Before we sleep tonight I bid of you that within your prayers we take a moment to share the same prayer, and that will be that His Holiness will see the truth of our love for the Lord."

Each man nodded and I knew it would be so.

CHAPTER THIRTEEN

The power of pure thoughts combined with love, commitment and passion is all encompassing. This is not only to the one who beholds this. It also radiates out within their words and actions. It reflects back upon them too so that their intention and glory grows and expands, which in turn brings more glory.

This was the greatest reward that my life would give. The more I knew my love of God and spirit, then the more I radiated this. In turn this brought to me a greater experience of this love, which inspired me to greater works. So that night with twelve of us united in our love, commitment and passion I would see one of the many times this reflection would come to bless us.

Pope Innocent had a restless start to his night. He lay in bed with his lamplight flickering and pondered over all that had been within his day. Then he replayed his meeting with me. The Cardinal of Sabina had been right; these men were balanced and true. Even just shaking hands with us had been enough to let him know we were at least sane and reasonable.

He took a deep breath. We were not heretics and we were showing respect for the church. These were all qualities to be approved of. When he prayed and asked for God's guidance he heard a simple "Yes" that he could not deny.

Then another side of the Pope came in. It was the part of him that was the administrator, the custodian of the church's values and rules. It was the part of his role he liked the least, yet was the most important in maintaining some order and sensibilities. It was a constant struggle to keep this in balance with the faith that had drawn him to the priesthood to begin with.

He could not simply and so quickly ordain us as an order. That would make him seem flippant and easily persuaded to accept anyone who made way to Rome. He had to remain, at least in appearance, to be strong and in command of the church.

It was then that his faith spoke up. Its whispers had been growing stronger lately.

"You want to make change and you can. God granted you this power to shape the church so bring it back to the beauty you know it can behold."

The Pope rubbed his brow. He still had until the morning to make a final decision and it was with immense relief that he finally felt sleep come upon him.

It was as though the dream came immediately. Pope Innocent was standing outside facing the church of Saint John. He looked about him and saw the square was empty of all the beggars which made him feel alarmed and concerned. Then he heard a rumble and looked to the church to see it was shifting in place.

Great cracks were appearing in the walls and pieces of the wooden carvings that adorned it were coming loose and falling to the cobblestones. He gasped and put his hands to his mouth. The Pope knew he was helpless to stop its imminent collapse.

Then I appeared by his side, putting my hand on his shoulder and smiling. I said nothing but walked towards the crumbling church. Innocent called out to me, hoping I would stop before I was injured but I kept walking and was soon by the wall of the church. I put my hands up, pushing at the wall and the movement of the church slowed.

Then another of my men passed by the Pope and joined me, also holding up the church and its decay stopped even more. Then another, and another of my order came to stand around the church to support its walls. Soon it was stable and the Pope walked to thank us.

As he approached the church, his dream was broken by his curtains being thrown wide by a servant. He opened his eyes to see that dawn was beginning and he rose to make way for the first prayers of the day. The Pope played out his part as he did every morning; reading a passage of the bible that had been chosen the previous day, leading the usual prayers and asking for God's guidance for the day that would unfold.

All the while though the energy of his dream was upon him. He looked up at one point, almost searching to see if there were any cracks upon the church walls or any sign of decay, but he knew this was futile. Such dreams were not so literal, despite the story it had shown. Pope Innocent knew what God had been showing him.

When we appeared before him only a few hours later, he did not share his dream. That would be something very few would ever know of until many years later as the Pope's final days were upon him. Instead we were most graciously informed that we had God and the church's blessings to continue our work. We would not be ordained as a recognised order as yet though.

"You have much to show us as to how you will conduct yourselves and how you will teach. Continue on as you have been, organise your order, gather more worshippers who embrace the Lord and his word, then we shall talk of ordination," he said.

We left though with two clear symbols of his validation. We carried with us a letter of decree that would prove our meeting. However we would also wear a very immediate and strong measure of our worth. The Pope approved us to be tonsured.

This may seem trivial or small but it was a distinction that no priest took lightly, especially not myself, or any of my group. This simply meant we were to have our heads shaved, but leaving a circle of our own hair almost like a crown. We received this in honour of the suffering of Saint Peter who had his head shaved as punishment to attract ridicule and suffering. When the Lord Christ saw this he went to Peter and placed his hand upon his smooth scalp and in that moment his mocking and punishment was turned to respect and worthiness.

No man received the tonsure and was not moved by the story of its origins. Though we all knew that this was bestowed upon us by a man, we too knew it was another sign of God's blessing upon us. As Peter was to Jesus, so too would we now be to his work also.

As we made way back to Assisi, our smiles were broader and our songs louder. The tonsure made complete the image of a Franciscan as it would always be known; men furnished in simple brown hooded robes, a belt of plain cord around our waist, the most basic of sandals upon our feet and the shaved circle upon our head.

I remember looking upon our group as we walked back from Rome and feeling that sense of completion in what we had set out to achieve. Inside though I felt something more swell up. I knew this excursion, though it had completed much, was just the beginning. Despite all I had been through and that of all my men, it was little of what lay ahead. This delighted me no end.

I looked up to the sky, an eternal reminder of how vast the creations of God's work were and smiled.

"I am ready," I declared.

The eleven monks with me all stopped and looked upon me. Then they too looked to the sky. Instantly they knew that I was making a declaration to the heavens and our Lord.

"As am I," shouted Angelo to the sky.

"As am I," roared Edigio as he too looked up.

This was followed by nine more voices all proclaiming the same. When we were all complete, Angelo began to sing and we all joined him as we continued on our way.

CHAPTER FOURTEEN

Life continues on for us all. Some of us see into how it will be while others let it fall upon them. As a member of the former I respected the latter. I also knew my work with the Lord could bring many of these to know a life of awareness to live in the grace and love of God. For when we have clarity about our connection with spirit then we can shape our lives to be rich and fruitful.

I am certain that all people desire a life that is one of their choice and not that of fate or being a victim of circumstance. Many people choose paths of evil and deception simply because that will satisfy their urge to have control and break from the routine that society seems to place upon all of us. Thankfully there are many who seek lives based more in the light and with a heart filled with love.

I will not pretend that being a male didn't make my choice to break from family far easier than had I been female. In fact I am certain it may never have occurred. I looked about me at the roles we played based upon our gender and while I saw imbalance, I also saw the beauty of the difference and how it served humanity. What I saw and honoured above all else was that what we carried in our hearts was far more important than what was formed of our bodies. Faith and devotion was not decided by one's gender and nor should it be limited by it either.

It was our first Palm Sunday since we were received by the Pope and the plans for our Easter celebrations were filled with so much joy and anticipation. Angelo had the inspiration to recreate the arrival of Jesus into Jerusalem.

"Imagine that we could give people the sense of what that was like. It will be as though we are welcoming our Saviour here to our church as much as it will honour his story," he had proposed, grinning from ear to ear with excitement.

"What a glorious idea!" I agreed. "So you shall play our Saviour's part then?"

"Oh no, it should be you," he protested.

"Or what if it is our newest acolyte?" I suggested. "Like we are welcoming them as well?"

We both knew that every priest was worthy to play such a part and so we decided upon a ballot, with a name chosen at random. This was how Rufino was chosen to play the role.

Rufino came from one of the noble families of Assisi. His decision to join my church had only just been accepted by his family after our audience with the Pope. It made for much better stories when a parent could brag about such an event as opposed to relaying that he was simply in the hills preaching to farmers.

"The Pope even took each one's hand!" his father would boast and people would raise their eyebrows and emit a sound to acknowledge that this was indeed impressive.

Rufino's father was telling this story to his brother one day whilst visiting the brother's home. His brother added stories that he had heard about other people who had met the Pope, while the women talked about the fashions in Rome. One person though remained quiet as the tales and speculations were bounced back and forth across the dinner table.

Clare ached to hear more about Rufino's adventures but she did not care for such stories which to her were just the superficial embellishments used to make entertaining talk.

She knew the strength it had taken Rufino to defy his upbringing. She knew how much wealth and comfort he had turned his back upon. Even more so, Clare knew the ache to shed the weight of a family and its expectations upon you. She did not care that Rufino had met the Pope. Clare wanted to know what Rufino's life was like now: was he happy, did his heart swell with joy and was he filled with love? She stabbed at her food, not listening to anything being said until something finally made her look up.

"...and he has been chosen to represent Jesus in a parade for Palm Sunday. They say he was chosen by a chance lottery but surely the Lord wouldn't just let anyone play the part of his son!"

Clare dropped her fork and the sound as it hit the plate made everyone turn and look upon her as a maid ran to help. Rufino's father wasn't going to have any attention taken from him though and continued on.

"Of course I will be attending mass here in town though. I do feel we owe it to the established church to support them."

Clare had picked up her fork and now wanted to hurl it across the table at her uncle and shout "You are a fool!" but as always she remembered her place.

"Oh to have been born a man," she thought to herself and sighed.

"Oh to have been born a man..."

It was a phrase that often made its way into Clare's thoughts. It was there when her maid pulled her corset ribbons tighter. It was there when she saw her brothers walk freely about town at their will. It was there when her mother's hand stung her cheek with a slap as she refused to receive a suitor.

"One day you will see the errors of your ways," her mother hissed. "Keep refusing and no one will call upon you. Then you can spend your final days praying upon the charity of others and not have the comfort of being cared for by your children and within a home provided by a husband."

Clare wanted to smirk when she heard those words, but the fire of her mother's hand upon her face made her think better.

"So that is all I am? A guarantee of care and company in someone's old age?" she thought to herself and a heat rose up within her that then made her want to laugh.

Clare made her way to the parlour as soon as her mother had left her. This was her haven, even when family were there too. The parlour was where the family said their nightly prayers. It was the time when Clare felt safe and peaceful, regardless of anything the day had held for her. Often when she felt idle or lost during the day she would find her way here also to connect with that sense of grace.

Upon a small table against a wall, a makeshift altar had been created. It was adorned with a crucifix as well as statues of Jesus and some saints. When Clare knelt before it, it was as though the rest of the world fell away.

Clare would begin with prayers. They were the standard ones that she would have said with her family or within the church at Sunday mass. In the past her time in the parlour would have ended at that but in recent years something had changed. Clare found that as she finished the prayers and placed the rosary beads back upon the altar, she no longer felt that she was done. Instead she would remain upon her knees and simply be silent.

She would keep her eyes closed and with the words of her prayers now complete, her mind would revel in the silence of the room. At first it was just a relief to be free of her mother's constant demands and nagging, but as Clare allowed this silence more and more she felt something beyond the respite from her family: it opened up something within her.

At first it was quite novel to feel things within herself that she was sure no one else could feel but as she looked upon the statues before her on the altar she knew that she was not the first to experience such things.

Clare leaned forward and stared into the faces of all those figurines before her. Each one had an amazing story to tell. One had the greatest story ever told! Each one had started out humbly and in awe of the creator who had placed them upon this Earth.

Clare knew their stories well. She knew of their passion and commitment to serving God and humanity. That was when she heard the answer to the question she had asked of herself after her mother's lecture.

"I am a child of God. I am here to serve the Holy Spirit. For I am that I am!"

Within that moment Clare knew she was much more than a daughter or a sister. Clare knew that she was not just placed upon this Earth to marry and reproduce. Clare knew that story was not hers. She had one much grander to write.

When one allows their soul to speak to them thus it opens up communications a closed mind can never imagine. Clare now had a much bigger vision of life and how it would unfold. There was no fear of being old and alone, and the next slap from her mother did not sting as it had before.

"Go and pray!" her mother snapped. "Pray that God will give you some sense."

Clare smiled openly, knowing that God had given her every sense she needed. She did not care that her time spent praying was being mocked, as long as they did not stop her. Clare would do prayers before sunrise, mid morning, after lunch, before the evening meal and then again with her family.

"At least it makes her appear pious," sighed her mother to her father.

"I doubt piety attracts husbands," muttered her father.

"No it won't, but your dowry will. Thank God."

The more time and energy Clare gave to her prayer, the more the outside world faded away. Not that she was disconnected to what was happening around her. It was just that it didn't seem to matter or affect her so much anymore. Mocking comments didn't cut her nor did eye-rolling or pitiful glances.

"People are talking about you in town. Soon the only men who will call on you will be the old widowers or the wounded and simple," one of her sisters had told her as a truly concerned warning.

"Let them talk. Their lives must be so empty if my life is needed to entertain them," sighed Clare.

Clare's life was full with an inner connection and stream of wisdom that nothing outside of her would ever satisfy again. Her time of post prayer silence had become a time for her soul's sharing. She knew it as the Holy Spirit filling her, much as I had within my prison cell. Its energy made her heart full and warm. Its caress erased all fear and doubts. Then one day this expanded again.

It was late afternoon and Clare loved to pray as the sun began to set. There was something about the surrender of the sun at dusk that she could relate to. Clare also loved that she could begin with a room filled with sunshine and end with shadows and lamplight flickering around her.

The maid had just left the room after lighting the lamps. Clare hardly noticed her as she was so deep within her silent state communicating with the Holy Spirit. Then Clare heard a voice begin to speak her name softly. Imagining it was the maid needing to tell her something Clare opened her eyes and looked around but the maid was long gone.

Clare closed her eyes once more and sought the solace of spirit when the voice called her name again. She dove deep into its energy, knowing this was not the voice of spirit as it usually chose to speak with her.

"Who are you? Are you a demon to distract me?" Clare asked, desperate for some clarity.

The voice laughed softly. "No, my child. Open your eyes."

Clare opened her eyes and before her she saw the small statue of Mother Mary surrounded by a soft glow. Though her lips did not move it was as though she was now speaking.

"Do not fear me," Mary called to her.

"How could I fear you? I am born of you," answered Clare.

There were no more words between them that day but Clare sat and stared into the aura surrounding the icon and felt all the Holy Mother had to share. This continued until a maid tapped upon the door and let her know that dinner was ready. The glow around the figurine faded and Clare reached out to touch it. There was a gentle heat about it that she knew was nothing to do with the nearby lantern.

This new communication continued on and grew. It was not always Mary who connected with her. Sometimes it was Saint Peter or Paul, and after some time Jesus spoke with her as well.

Their words came as whispers through the soft light around them. Some days they made no sense but this did not sway Clare's faith in them or herself.

"I know my soul will understand in perfect time," she told them one day.

It was this refusal to submit to any doubts that allowed even more of the connection to flow. Soon Clare could see their small wooden chests expand and contract as though the icons were breathing. She was sure they also smiled at her and this made her heart sing with joy.

Clare also knew not to share what was happening with anyone. Now this may seem that she was simply avoiding more judgement and ridicule, which in part was true, but even more so she knew that the doubts and fears of others could distract her. Even when her youngest sister Agnes began to ask her questions and join her in prayers, she did not falter. Clare understood how sacred her new world was and that it needed to be protected.

The day Rufino's father came to visit, Clare was before her altar and looking upon Jesus. His chest rose and sank. His eyes opened wide for her. Clare looked at his hand with their palms facing outwards and saw red marks begin to appear. They grew larger and larger; soon it was as though they dripped down his fingers. Across his forehead more red appeared and seeped down his face.

"Your wounds..." Clare whispered.

"Yes," replied Jesus and the red disappeared.

Later Clare sat at the dinner table and as she listened to her uncle, in her mind she saw the stigmata appear over and over. Often within such reflection the message or key of what had been shared would be revealed. As soon as her uncle spoke of Rufino being chosen to represent Christ in the Palm Sunday enactment she knew what she needed to know.

As she lay in bed that night saying her final prayers, Jesus appeared by her bedside and for the first time Clare was actually scared. It was one thing for a small statue to glow before you but to have a man appear beside your bed in the dark was another.

"Now you choose to fear me?" he smiled and Clare relaxed. "It's time to live your truth," he said.

Clare nodded but within her a voice called out, "How?"

"Do what you know to be right and all will be revealed," was the response and then her visitor was gone.

Clare didn't dream so much these days but that night her visions were so complete and active that she woke still tired. This did not bother her so much for within her dreams she knew what to do.

✦ CHAPTER FIFTEEN

Her dream began with Clare walking to our church. Clare looked down and saw she had no shoes or stockings. Her dress was a simple and modest shift and her hair flowed loose and free.

"I am like a beggar," she thought but then it shifted.

"I am free," she sang and began to skip as she made her way.

Clare arrived at our church and pushed through the crowd which had gathered outside. She had to force her way with all her might as no one seemed to want to make room for her. In their hands the throng waved huge palm leaves and Clare wondered where they had gathered the fronds from. Then she laughed at why she was even thinking this.

Eventually she got to the front and was looking upon the avenue of people and greenery. They were all singing a hymn she did not recognise as they looked to the left. As Clare turned her head the same way she saw a group of monks making their way through the crowd. They were singing and dancing along with the gathering. Some played small drums, others had bells or harps. Their smiles were broad and of limitless joy.

As they danced past her Clare almost ran forward to join them but a great cheer from the crowd stopped her and she looked back down the avenue. Coming now was Jesus looking just as he had when he appeared by her bedside. He rode upon the finest donkey she had ever seen, being led by a monk. Jesus smiled at everyone, waving his hand to acknowledge his warm welcome.

Someone ran to him and he called for the donkey to be stopped so he could place his hand upon the woman's head. He leant down and whispered something to her as she began to weep. Then he began to move forward again.

When the donkey came closer to her, Clare looked up into Jesus' eyes and saw a bright light coming from them and then she noticed the soft glow around his body.

"It is always there," she thought and Jesus nodded.

"Clare," a voice called to her and she looked to the monk who was leading the donkey. He stopped just before her and beckoned to her to come to him.

As she walked close he held out the lead of the donkey.

"It is your turn now," he said.

Clare looked up at Jesus who smiled and nodded. She stepped forward, took the leather cord into her hand and began to lead the donkey through the people. They had not stopped cheering. Their palm fronds were still aloft and swaying. Clare could barely see the sky through them and she continued to walk as though this was the most natural thing she had ever done.

When Palm Sunday arrived Clare was ready and well prepared for what she would do. As her family gathered within the home before leaving for the service at the Assisi cathedral she sent a maid to explain that she was ill and would not join them.

Her mother tugged at her gloves as she glared up the stairs towards Clare's room.

"Oh leave her! She says enough prayers for a year within a week. God will not miss her today," laughed her father.

This was not what concerned her mother. Now she would have to receive the patronising glances and smirks of the other women when they saw Clare absent. There was already enough idle gossip without this to add to it. Her mother tied the ribbon of her hat, then she began to practice her fake smile as well as prepare the curt but polite explanations she would have to deliver.

Clare remained in bed listening for the sounds of the carriages to fade away. When she heard the bustle of the maids going about their daily chores though was when she knew the family were truly gone. She jumped from bed and began to dress herself.

No corset today. No hair braided and coiled around her head. No perfumes or powders dabbed upon her. Clare put on her plainest dress, tied her hair back with a ribbon and slipped on some comfortable walking shoes. Then she listened for the maids to head back to the kitchen and laundry before she ran down the stairs and out of the house.

She didn't stop running then either. Even though everyone in the neighbourhood would be at church and only servants were left to see her, Clare kept going until she was well away of the houses and within the foothills. Once there she stopped and leaned against a tree to catch her breath.

Her running had loosened her ribbon and it had fallen some time ago, leaving her hair flowing across her shoulders. Clare also realised she had forgotten stockings and her feet were red where her shoes had rubbed upon them. She slipped her shoes off, leaving them beside the tree and continued on.

If Clare was in any doubt as to how to find us, we were making sure this was not to be so. She could hear the music before she could even see the church. The wind carried the sound as though it was guiding her.

Then the crowd revealed itself high upon the hillside; it was just as in her dream.

She could see the palm fronds swaying. She could hear the music and the cheering. Clare began to run once more and was soon upon the edge of the gathering. Pushing up upon her toes she tried to look over the shoulders to see what was happening.

"Here little one, make your way to the front," said a man and pushed her into the throng.

Clare had no choice now but to keep barging her way through to the front, if only to have air to breathe. Emerging out the other side she saw across from her a matching crowd and realised this was indeed the rec-reation of the road into Jerusalem. Before she knew it, Rufino appeared upon the donkey, smiling and waving to all. There was no monk to lead him as he drove the animal himself.

"Rufino! Rufino!" Clare called out as he passed but he could not hear her amongst the singing and cheering.

As he made way the avenue collapsed behind him as the crowd now formed the procession to the church. Clare was now carried along with them until Rufino arrived at the front door and they all stopped. Here I was to greet our Jesus, welcoming him and inviting him to bless our chapel. Rufino stepped off the donkey and turned to the crowd, raising his hands high in the air. The people let out an almighty cheer and Rufino grinned from ear to ear.

"Children of God, you bless me with your warmth and hospitality. I call upon our eternal father, the grand creator to bless this church and all who will pray within it. Now let us go inside and celebrate the love and joy of his words," he called out.

There was one more ear-shattering cheer and then all fell into si-lence as they made way into the church. Rufino walked to the altar and stood to face down the aisle. He still did not see Clare as she walked along the back wall to stand in the corner almost as though to hide her presence.

"Oh no, child!" an older man said as he saw her lean against the wall. "Come sit here."

He motioned to a pew. Clare nodded and took her seat, all the while not taking her eyes off of Rufino. As she sat and her heart calmed she noticed something that was new about him but somehow familiar. Clare slowed her breath and closed her eyes. When she opened them again she could now see what she had sensed. There was a delicate white glow around her cousin, much the same as when she looked upon the statue of Jesus at home.

Clare fell back into the pew and sighed. It was a sigh so loud that the woman next to her turned to look upon her with concern. However when she saw the smile upon Clare's face she smiled also.

"It is like arriving at the home of a friend, is it not?" the woman whispered as she leaned over to Clare.

Clare nodded and a gentle tear fell from her eye. The woman grabbed her hand and held it tight.

"Welcome home," she said and then Rufino began the mass.

Rufino spoke as though he was Jesus standing before the people. He did not speak as though someone else placed the words upon his tongue but that they were his own expression in that moment.

"This is what it must have been like to see our Lord speak at the mount," the woman said to Clare but never took her eyes from Rufino for a second.

Rufino still in his role as Jesus blessed the congregation.

"Go now with your hearts full. Go now and know that I am always with you," he said with his arms outstretched.

"Praise be to you!" called out a parishioner.

"As it is also to you," Rufino responded.

With that the mass was ended.

The woman squeezed Clare's hand one last time. "Come to our home for lunch and rest. We have fresh figs and the finest wine that my husband makes. All from our gardens."

Clare shook her head. "Perhaps another time. I feel I shall sit within this sacred space some more."

The woman nodded and let go of Clare's hand. She stood to leave but leant and kissed Clare upon the forehead before making her way. Now alone except for the monks who walked the church straightening pews and sweeping, Clare closed her eyes and prayed.

It was the sort of prayer with no words that she always fell into. The kind silent space where the Lord or the saints would talk to her, but she could hear nothing, only feeling their love and guidance. Clare opened her eyes and there I stood before her smiling.

She had no idea of my name but she knew my face. I was the monk who had handed her the lead of the donkey in her dream.

Clare put her hands to her face and began to sob.

It wasn't the first time I had welcomed a new parishioner and had them reduced to tears. I would wait patiently for them to finish knowing that it was just an expression of their joy and relief to be back with the Lord. When I stood waiting for Clare's tears to stop though I felt something much deeper. It was like the sense I had when a new acolyte or monk was here to join the brotherhood.

I quickly took a deep breath and looked back to our statue of Jesus upon his cross. I could usually feel within him some clarity when I could not capture my own but I sensed no shift in this. I looked back upon Clare as she gathered herself and wiped her face upon her sleeves.

"I had a dream. I was here and I saw Jesus upon the donkey. It was not Rufino but our Lord himself. He smiled at me—and—and—then you were there. You were leading the donkey and you handed me his lead. You said it was my turn," she let out the words quickly as though it was a relief to have them leave her mouth.

For the first time in a long time I was lost for words. I did not doubt her vision in the slightest. Many men came to me with stories of dreams that led them to join us. This was the first time a woman had done so and as she looked to me for affirmation or rejection I still could not find any words.

"Clare?"

It was Rufino now back in his brown monk robes after shedding his white clothing. He had come to look for me to pray after the service and prepare for the next.

"I thought it was you. How wonderful to see you here," he said with a smile but then his face grew dark as he saw the way she was dressed and her bare feet upon the stone floor. "Does your family know you are here?"

With that Clare began to cry again as she shook her head.

I took a deep breath. "Let us go back to the monastery. I feel there is much we need to talk about," I said as I reached for Clare's hand to lead her out of the chapel.

"How did you get here?" Rufino now asked but I hushed him with a simple raised hand.

We walked silently back to the monastery. Clare was between us; her posture slouched with the appearance of someone who was exhausted. Rufino from time to time would place his hand upon her shoulder.

At the monastery we took Clare into one of the small rooms used for reading. I could call it a library but that would conjure something far grander in your mind. There were a handful of books and most of them were simply bibles. There were a few hard chairs and two small desks. Clare looked about her and was momentarily confused as to where we had taken her.

"What is this room?" she asked.

"It is where we can sit to study the word of the Lord," Rufino explained and wanted to laugh. "Not quite like the sitting rooms we have in our family homes is it?"

With this Clare laughed as she shook her head and her energy lifted.

We sat down with no table between us and smiled at Clare.

"Tell me everything," I said simply.

Clare lifted her head, took a deep breath and squared her shoulders. Then she began and we did not stop her until she finished with the words "…and when I saw your face Francis, I just knew my life is now to work with you and your order."

"You do know we have no women here?" Rufino said his brow furrowed.

Clare rolled her eyes at him but then caught the amused smile on my face and composed herself.

"Forgive me Francis but I find it hard to believe my gender should limit my dedication and service to the Lord."

With this Clare folded her arms and looked at her cousin.

"I did not mean to offend you. Your gender does not limit anything about you when it comes to honour and service to God. It is just that there are many orders for women that you could join," Rufino explained.

Clare closed her eyes and sighed deeply. I looked at her arms tightly wrapped around her and then to her bare feet.

"What happened to your shoes?" I asked.

"I shed them to make my journey without getting blisters. In my speed to get here I forgot my stockings and the shoes made my feet ache with their rubbing," she explained.

"Well we must go find them for you," I insisted before adding, "women are rather fond of their shoes. I imagine you must be missing them."

It was a tease of huge magnitude laced with just the right dose of patronising tone needed to elicit the response I hoped for.

Clare turned and glared at me and within that expression was all I needed to know. Her words that followed were but a delightful confirmation.

"I am not fond of anything which adorns me. I will never miss my shoes nor anything of the life I have walked away from. There is nothing so important as that which I hold inside!"

I was immediately taken back to that moment before the magistrate when I had shed the last threads of my family life. I turned to Rufino who had a look of sheer horror after watching his cousin speak to me this way and I smiled.

"Well Rufino, I imagine it is time we began a female order to accompany the brotherhood," I announced.

CHAPTER SIXTEEN

It was sixteen days later when our female order doubled in numbers with the addition of Clare's younger sister Agnes. However it was sixteen days filled with much that Clare's family needed to come to terms with.

When Clare disappeared that Sunday it seemed her parents could barely care.

"This is just another way to get attention," her mother declared then sighed. "I imagine she will return saying she had some visions and with great prophecies for us all."

When three days passed though and there was no sign of their daughter the indifference was replaced with genuine concern. Clare's mother fell ill and as Agnes stood at the doorway of her parent's bedroom watching her mother lie upon her bed, one hand held to her forehead and the other to her belly, she took a deep breath and made way to the salon.

Once here she knelt before the altar and prayed in the only way she knew how. She called out to God asking for his protection of her sister and then repeated this plea to each saint she could think to name. Then she fell silent and began to cry.

"I am safe and well."

Agnes knew immediately it was the voice of Clare calling out to her and her tears stopped.

It was this very same day that Rufino went to Clare as she helped tend our kitchen garden.

"This must be interesting for you," he laughed as he watched her pull weeds and straighten some bean trails upon their frame.

Clare screwed up her nose at him and squared her shoulders. "So you imagine having servants tend to me my whole life makes it 'interesting' to now contribute to my community?"

Rufino took a breath and made note to himself to avoid any attempts at humour with his cousin from now on.

"Clare, it is apparent you are dedicated to being a part of our order as well as to your own life with spirit. We must send word to your family," he began.

"NO!"

It was short, loud and emphatic, bringing Rufino's speech to a momentary halt. He closed his eyes and took another breath.

"Clare, we all sent word to our families. Regardless of the outcome, it must be done."

"WHY?"

"Because it allows them the relief to know we are safe. It gives them some sense of completion," he paused. "It is the declaration of our choice. It allows us to be free to do the work we have chosen."

Clare stopped what she was doing and looked down at the ground.

"I want that freedom," she said softly.

Rufino nodded. "We all want it but until we clear our old ties and obligations, then we are not free to be who we want to be. No matter how hard that final detachment may seem."

Clare nodded and looked up, offering her cousin a half-hearted smile. It was enough for Rufino though. He returned the nod and went to the monastery to write the letter to his aunt and uncle.

Clare's father's hands began to shake as he read the letter when it arrived in Assisi. His face turned red and then he found himself crushing the paper between his fingers. His mouth spoke some profanities and then the letter was hurled upon the floor. He grabbed at his chest then rubbed his forehead.

This was beyond anything that he could imagine happening with any of his children. Part of him had prayed one of his own sons might join Rufino and become something of a local celebrity as many of the men in my order had, thanks to the bragging of their parents.

But for a daughter to leave his home and join us? Dear God, it was barely worth thinking about. What had she been doing for three days surrounded by dozens of men? He didn't care that we were men of God. All men had urges and he knew of the rumours of even the highest of priests with women in their parish.

His blood ran cold. Even if he brought her back now, if word was to get out about this, his daughter would be worth no more than dirt. The family had survived the talk of her eccentricities. It had hidden her disappearance with talk of illness, but this would be impossible to brush over or make excuse for.

There was only one solution. He would make way to our community and gather his daughter before this escalated and people found out. Clare's father knew he could not do this alone and called upon his three sons. Then the four of them made way to one more home before riding up into the hills.

When they arrived at Rufino's family home, Rufino's father came running to greet them.

"How wonderful! All four men of your family here to visit. Come, come. We will share some food and wine," he beckoned them inside but as he saw the sombre looks upon their faces his tone shifted. "What is it? Are you here with bad news? Oh no..." he made the sign of the cross and put his hands together as though to pray.

Clare's father slid down from his horse and walked to him, grabbing at his shirt and pulling him close. Then in the darkest of voices he did indeed share what he considered bad news.

"My daughter has left our home to join those—those decadents in the hills. This is because of your son. This is because of all you spoke of him and the glory you have given him. My sons and I will go now to bring her home. I am giving you a chance for redemption by asking you to join me and make what your family have wronged right once more."

Rufino's father reached for the hand upon his shirt and pulled it off him, throwing it back at his brother.

"My son was called by God to serve him. He listened to that call and now serves our Lord in the most glorious way. Your daughter has now heard the call too. I will never interfere in the work of the Lord," he stepped back cautiously, eyeing his nephews as he did so but none made move to approach him.

Clare's father caught his breath and his shoulders heaved. He nodded his head but his face was locked in a grimace.

"You have spoken your piece and declared your intentions. Know this though; we shall never speak again."

As Clare's family rode away, Rufino's father contemplated the prospect of never conversing with his brother again. Surprisingly he felt no remorse or regret for the outcome of standing his ground. Instead all he felt to do was pray for Clare.

When his uncle and cousins arrived at the monastery Rufino knew it was not a visit to be filled with joy or any courtesies. Regardless he walked with his head held high and his hands resting gently upon his forearms within his sleeves. He did not offer any greeting but took a deep breath and smiled at his relatives.

"How dare you smile at me?" his uncle sneered as he leapt down from his horse and approached him with his sons close behind. "Get my daughter now and place her upon a horse to return home."

"I cannot do that," replied Rufino softly and within his chest he felt his heart begin to beat a little bit faster.

Other brothers of the order began to gather around him. They had heard the uncle's tone and volume, and made way calmly to support Rufino. One silently slipped away to call me.

This was not the first time that a family had confronted us to demand the return of a child. However it was the first time that it had occurred for a daughter rather than a son. We knew instinctively that this would be far different.

Clare's father raised his voice once more and looked beyond the group of monks as he now yelled out, "Come Bernardone! You coward! Too weak to live your family honour and now too weak to face the father of a girl you have molested."

Rufino gasped. "Uncle, you cannot accuse anyone here of such things," he hissed.

"It is alright Rufino," I said loudly as I approached. "It is perfectly understandable that such accusations should be made. This is a father's love speaking. Surely such a love would speak with concern and care for the child and not for the standing of the father. That is where such comments come from. Do they not?"

The father's face turned red and he started to shake as I held my gaze firm to his eyes.

"You will never have children to understand a father's love and protection," he snarled.

"I have the love of the Lord and that is all I need to understand," I replied calmly.

The father lurched forward to hit me but one of his sons grabbed at him, pulling him back. I may be a priest who they hated but I was still a priest and to assault me was unacceptable.

Clare could hear her father's yelling and hid around a corner nearby to watch and listen. She knew her father was all bluster and would give up soon enough. However when she saw him ready to attack me she came running.

"How dare you!" she yelled.

Her father straightened himself and he pushed the son away. Then he pointed at Clare.

"Get upon a horse now and make ready to return home," he finished by pointing to his horse.

"NO!"

It was the response that every man standing there was expecting. Even her father, yet all it did was evoke even more anger in the man. He flew at his daughter and began to beat her. It was so quick that Clare was upon her knees and received several blows before anyone could react.

In fact it was as though for the rest of us time somehow slowed

106

down. I recall running to her, yet it felt like my legs weighed of lead and simply could not move as fast as I needed them to. As this happened my eyes stayed upon Clare. I saw her look up at her father and as his fists rained upon her, she looked at him squarely and her eyes did not once blink nor did her body flinch or her arms seek to protect herself. She received each blow with more courage and strength than I ever saw of any man.

As we pulled her father away he replaced his angry blows with vicious words.

"Whore! Useless wench! Stay and spread your legs for these heathens! I pray they will infect you with all their illnesses! Birth their bastard children!"

"Each word was like a key turning in a lock. I felt as though each insult and curse was another part of my freedom being gifted to me," Clare told me later.

I nodded my head remembering the bile my father had spat at me before the magistrate in Assisi.

"And the blows? You did not baulk once," I said.

Clare smiled. "As soon as his eyes met mine I heard an angel say that he would beat me. I told them I was ready for that and to make me strong for whatever I was about to receive. As I knelt there I felt that angel take all the pain and anger that my father wished to gift to me. I felt not a thing."

Indeed the next day there was not one bruise or graze upon her body. In fact Clare looked as healthy and complete as she ever did.

"This is a miracle," I said as I looked upon her face recalling the blows I had seen it receive.

"This is no miracle. This is faith and love," she declared.

CHAPTER SEVENTEEN

Clare's father returned home and was still shaking with such anger that he could not speak. Instead he collapsed into a lounge chair in the salon and the eldest of the sons spoke to the mother.

"She will not return," he said simply then looked to his father momentarily before lowering his voice to continue. "And Father made it clear that she would not be welcome if she decided to do so in the future."

"She is their whore now," the father yelled out as he grabbed at his chest.

The mother began to sob.

Agnes stood in the hallway, close enough to listen, yet with enough distance to sneak away quickly should someone walk out of the salon. She heard the news and her father's insult. Her heart both sang and sunk at the same time.

She knew she must go see her sister but also knew that to do this so soon would cause even more grief for everyone.

"I will wait and let the Lord guide me, " she decided.

Easter in their home was a sombre occasion.

"I cannot bear to go to church on Sunday," the mother said as she shuddered imagining the looks she would receive.

Word had indeed gotten out within Assisi about Clare's addition to our community.

"Dear God! Now he is taking women as well!" was the most frequent comment.

None were surprised that Clare was the first female to join us.

"Her poor parents. Where did they go wrong?"

Agnes heard this one day as she walked through the markets and her blood became hot. She turned fast upon her heels and walked up to the gossiping women.

"They did nothing wrong. They simply had a daughter who was willing to hear and listen to our Lord."

With that she walked away as quickly as she had sprung herself upon the women, leaving them with mouths agape.

Agnes prayed each day but did so in her room. Her father had caught her at the altar in the salon and upturned the table, scattering candles and statues around Agnes as she knelt. Hot wax landed upon her dress just missing her bare hand.

"Go and do some needlework," her father spat. "There will be no more prayers within this house. God abandoned us in letting your sister be led astray and so we shall abandon him."

He may as well have stuck a knife into Agnes' chest. The grief this comment evoked within her heart made her want to cry out in agony. She reached around her to pick up the statues. Many of them were broken and she wept as she saw this.

Agnes lifted up Mother Mary, now in two pieces. She looked into the holy mother's face.

"Please forgive him," she cried.

Agnes took the statues both broken and intact to her room and hid them within a chest that sat under her bed.

"I will bring you out when it is safe. I promise," she said to the saints as she gently placed them within their new home.

Agnes found few occasions to do so before the Lord gave her clear passage to join us.

"You will go with the maids to market today," her mother announced one morning. "They seem intent on buying the lowest of goods for the highest of prices. Some family eyes upon them are needed to set this right and perhaps show them the standard of food we expect to be served in a noble house."

Agnes nodded and curtsied to accept this responsibility but inside she cringed and sighed.

"This will take hours and I will have to endure the glances of the other nobles...."

Then something shifted inside her and it was as though another voice replaced her first thought.

"Abandon the maids as soon as you can and it will be half a day before anyone knows you are missing."

Agnes knew this was the voice of God providing her the chance she had asked for.

"And to think my small mind would have let me think today would be otherwise."

It was a wonderful lesson Agnes would share over and over.

"Keep your heart full and dedicated to God and you will never miss any opportunity he will send you!"

So as Agnes and the two maids approached the markets she called for them to stop. Then she placed a coin in the palm of each girl.

"This is how today will occur," she began and the maids listened and nodded in agreement as she set out her plan.

The servants continued to market and bought some fine fare while bargaining with much success. When they returned home they gave the most perfect story to the lady of the house.

"When we finished at market, Miss Agnes sought to visit her friend Amelia and sent us along home," explained the maid just as Agnes had asked her to. It was a perfect story that absolved the maids and would not arouse any suspicion until Agnes failed to return by nightfall.

By the time the story was spoken Agnes was sitting holding hands with Clare while I looked on.

"This is not something that can begin with anything but complete dedication," I said expecting a harsh look from Clare, but her gaze remained upon her sister.

Agnes looked to me. "I know. I have had that set before me, as I shall show to those that follow."

There were many gifts that were granted to our order by the addition of the sisterhood. We now had the freedom for either sex to serve the Lord with us, but more than this we gained a balance that we did not even realise we were missing.

I had grown up with such a strong story for how each sex served humanity and what role they played. Men were strong and providers, women were soft and were carers. However now with our sisterhood as part of our community my ideals about women began to shift. I saw those roles begin to blur and it was magnificent.

Clare and Agnes had shown a strength very few men could ever know or understand in defying their families and society. Yes, many women served in nunneries across Europe and this was a role placed upon them by families seeking some sort of standing with God or the church. Many were placed simply so they were one less mouth to feed or because there was no dowry or beauty sufficient to attract a husband.

Some women found faith and connection while they served, finding blessings in being shed from their families or because there simply was no other sense in why their life had become such. Very few chose the vocation and servitude of their own volition and those who did were looked upon with wariness, as many did so to escape from lives filled with violence and other abuses.

As such many nunneries were simply houses of regret, avoidance or a place to reclaim a woman's power. This did not fare well for any connection to God to be nurtured to its fullest.

Our beautiful sisterhood was founded on love and integrity. Though many came to us with family chasing close behind this soon faded. Each woman, no matter their age or their standing came to us as free souls with absolute love for the Lord in their hearts. Even more so they came to us to live this life with love and honour for themselves. We found out that those, which did not have this intention, would soon be on their way.

"I have to sweep floors? But where are the servants?" one young girl asked on her first day.

Clare sighed and pushed the broom into her hand.

"We are all servants," she said plainly and forced a smile across her face.

When Clare came to check upon her progress she found the broom leaning against a wall and the young girl nowhere to be found.

Each sister who remained came to us in their own founded strength and commitment. Most had stories like Clare and Agnes, of hearing voices that they realised were divine. Of sensations that they had felt since childhood that they knew were beyond those of this world.

"I have an angel who has been with me since birth," one girl explained. "I have trusted her implicitly and she guided me here."

I will not say that my brotherhood was without grace, but the women held within them a grace that was undefinable but distinctly of their own. You could sense it within them before they even asked to remain as part of the order. You could see it like a glow radiating from them and even as I spoke mass I could look out and tell that another woman amongst the congregation was there to begin her service.

This grace was inexplicably aligned to the divine feminine; the holy motherhood that we believed was embodied in Mary. These women knew it was more than just a story about a young virgin chosen to birth Our Saviour. They knew they embodied an energy that was eternal and that held healing, completion and balance.

The beauty of this is that though they held it, they could not form this into words. It was something none of them could articulate. The blessing was that they chose to live it and those who sought their counsel or company would experience it without lecture or explanation.

To the outside world many saw the brotherhood as active, always travelling and on pilgrimage, organising masses and service, building new sanctuaries; while the sisters were quiet and still within their domain, moving quietly, doing gentle needlework or caring for the ill. For those who looked deeper or felt into our truth, they would see a balance that was of God and even more so the completion that he wishes us to live in.

There is no dark without light. There is no joy without knowing pain. This is the way of experience in life as we have always known and how I was taught. It is a very old way to teach acceptance and guide people to living a life of faith through fear of punishment or retribution. Contrasts and duality have served religion well.

Within our community though we took the old story of male and female and we turned it into a story of wholeness. We celebrated our differences while embracing that at our core we were of the same love and honour. It became like a dance of energies that made each order even grander so that when people came to be with us it entered their awareness and transformed their own story of their role as male or female.

A life built on faith, love and honour incurs a grace that becomes an inherent joy for choosing such a path.

CHAPTER EIGHTEEN

Over the years our community grew at a rate never known by any other religious order before. We sent missions to establish new communities all around Italy and my heart swelled to know this new way of connecting with Christ and our Creator was being embraced by even more people.

One day I knelt within the private sanctuary we had built for our priests so I could give thanks for this expansion of our work. The sanctuary was a small chapel that was at the far end of a corridor in our private dormitories. It was octagonal in shape and as you walked in it felt like the space opened around you, and yet embraced you at the same time.

Each of the seven walls that were not of the door to enter held a large window of clear glass so that the glory our Lord's creation could be seen. It also meant that anyone praying here could be observed and that was celebrated as there was no shame in private prayer. In fact it inspired it of others.

I loved to come here after my breakfast for I knew at this time the sun would pour its light within all the windows. It would slice into the room with the glass turning it into beams that became warm and held colours that were delightful.

A glorious statue of Jesus stood facing the doorway and the light from the window behind created a glow around him like an enormous halo. Then it would cast a shadow before him within which a pillow for kneeling upon to pray would wait for us.

I would love to stop and look at the play of light before I knelt. There was something magical in the way this occurred each day when the sun was not hindered by clouds. I would take a deep breath and peer out each window in turn looking at the trees and noting their current state - full of lush greenery or delicate orange and brown leaves about to fall or they could be barren and awaiting new life.

It reminded me that each day I needed to stop and take note of where my heart and spirit were. Was I full of the love and glory of the Lord? Was I empty and seeking redemption? Was I allowing the Holy Spirit to fill me and express through my work?

Each day I would take time to feel into my current state. What words and thoughts were driving me? Was my faith still strong as an ox? And it was this moment that made my spirit stronger and more complete. For each time I did this I recognised the original commitment I had made to my connection to God within the cold damp walls of my prison cell.

This could take barely a minute of my time and yet it was something that held with me all day and was within every breath I would take until the next morning. It was like an energetic stamp that would only fade if I allowed it to. It also made my personal energy as clear as crystal, so that when I knelt before our Saviour to commune with him I was in a space of perfect clarity and balance to receive his grace and gifts which were endless and of no limits.

So it was that I knelt before him this day to share my gratitude for allowing our order to flourish. I began with my usual prayers and then went to silence with just the rhythm of my breath and my heartbeat to communicate. In this space I sometimes heard words, other times I might be shown an image. On this day I saw a scene that delighted me.

I was onboard an immense ship and it dipped and rose up on the waves of a playful ocean. Each time the boat plunged down with a wave I could feel my stomach pulled down and yet it did not make me feel ill or scared. All I could do was look ahead in wonder as to where I was being carried to.

I asked no question of my Lord as to what this was about. There was no need. To be upon a ship meant only one thing and that was that it was time to take our order and faith to new lands far from not only Assisi but from Italy herself.

To fund passage to a foreign land was not of any consequence to our order. I will not lie about the money we continually received from offerings and tithes. However I never saw this as either fortune or wealth. I saw this as God's continual blessing for the work that we did and his endorsement that it should continue.

Our vow to poverty always remained. Such funds were never spent on luxuries. You would never find indulgent foods hidden in our pantries nor expensive furnishings within our quarters. All extra money was directed to feeding and clothing the poor, or it was used to establish other communities that in turn would attract their own abundance to support the needy of their congregation and surrounding area.

So when I took a small purse to pay my fare along with that of the three brothers who would accompany me, I did so with so much love and honour for our work and the integrity that we would express when we arrived in our new destination.

"Where shall we go?" asked Leo when I announced that I myself would be heading the mission.

"We shall go to the homeland of Our Saviour. I see no better place to shine our light. Then we shall fulfil pilgrimage to the holy sites as well."

Leo turned white. History, or rather the men who created the history of the Holy Lands, had painted a picture that was not so kind to Christians or any religion for that matter. I saw the look upon his face and smiled. I put my hand upon his shoulder and took a deep breath which inspired him to do also.

"Brother Leo, we go there as servants to Our Lord and his love. We do not go as soldiers or politicians. This will be our protection. Those who have suffered before us in these lands do not serve the truth of Our Lord. They went for power and glory. We go to shine love and grace. That will never be challenged."

Though I know Leo felt the truth of these words I could see something else within his eyes that still held a deep fear. It was also upon the faces of the other two brothers as we got to our feet after our final prayers at Assisi.

"Let us take our love and faith to new lands," I proclaimed as we left the church.

They all nodded silently but each one also carried a solemn expression.

We boarded the boat on the east coast in the morning after sleeping at a nearby inn. The night's sleep seemed to have only made the brother's fear steep stronger.

"I dreamt our boat was torn apart upon some rocks," Aguinus muttered over breakfast.

"I saw your severed head mounted upon a spike," said Bertrand as he looked glumly at me.

I said nothing in reply. Many of us had dreams that were prophetic and we encouraged their sharing for within these dreams were many messages. Today though I did not wish to hear any such divine messages within these dreams. I saw them as a way for the men to suitably let their fears find a voice. Yet inside I could not find any words, divinely gifted or otherwise, to dismiss them simply as this and something within me also now felt dark.

I pushed this aside and lifted my chin. "Come now! We shall return within a few weeks with glorious news to share with the brothers and sisters."

It was a vain attempt to rally some morale and I knew it.

As we boarded the boat I looked out to the ocean and imagined the distant shores we were headed towards. The sun shone fiercely that day which made the sea reflect it back as though the light was emitted from

117

the water itself. I had to shade my eyes and something within me made me feel as though I was about to enter a furnace.

I turned to the men. "Darkness will find any way to disrupt and distract us from our service and even worse, from the love of our Lord. These past few days it has come to play with all of us. I feel no embarrassment in admitting I too have fallen to its seduction. Just now as I looked upon the sky and the sea, I did not see the beauty of creation or impending adventure. I instead saw challenge and hardship. My love of the Lord and my trust in his protection will allay all these simple thoughts of man…."

I stumbled here and stopped speaking. Each brother kept nodding as they would when I spoke thusly but my pause and then abrupt ending was so out of character for how my speech normally flowed that they all looked at me with eyes wide. Any comfort I had just attempted to provide them vanished.

I opened my mouth again and tried, oh how I tried to keep speaking but the words could not form. Instead I turned and boarded the boat with the brothers silently behind me.

I always hated to use the term "devil" or even "darkness" when I spoke or served mass. To me using such tools for teaching or inspiring a connection to God seemed empty and of no purpose in guiding people to a life of grace. It was always one of the ways of the old church teachings that mystified me. To lead someone to God through fear always felt as though their faith was then built on unstable foundations.

You could see it within the congregation of any church that you walked into. These were the people who attended mass because to not do so could mean some divine punishment dished out to your life or worse, upon your death and for eternity in the afterlife. These were the people who walked through the doors of their cathedral with empty hearts and left just as unfulfilled because there was no deep connection to any words or prayers spoken there. To these people Jesus may as well have been a fairytale conjured to entertain and fill our days with some sense of order.

When we shared the love of God in bringing Jesus to us, and then shared the immense faith in which Jesus lived his life and then ended it, that gave people a very different story to take into their lives. They did not turn to God now from fear, but through inspiration gifted from Jesus' teachings.

A life built upon a foundation of love and joy is solid and allows a grandness to thrive upon it. A base of fear is always crumbling and needing maintenance. No true life can flourish upon it.

That day as I looked out and imagined stepping into a furnace I was reminded how easy it could be to fall back to those thoughts based upon fear and the old stories of hell and the devil. However there was something deeper than this that we were all experiencing. It was a new feeling and none of us could shake it off, but our sense of service and our commitment, as well as what was now my undoubtable stubbornness, allowed us to ignore it.

Aguinus turned white as soon as we boarded and grew whiter as the boat launched. As we began to sail I saw him so pale that I imagined it could go no further. Then he turned green and ran towards the back of the vessel to vomit. I stayed where I was at the side of the ship looking ahead. There was nothing to be done to help him and I did not want to be distracted from my own centre lest I miss any messages from Holy Spirit as to what was ahead.

It soon became apparent that there was nothing to hear or feel. I pushed hard into that space within but that is futile, for to force this communication negates the very nature of which it is born. Instead I noticed the ship began to dip and rise just as it had within my vision and I smiled.

The smile was short-lived as I realised that apart from this very predictable behaviour of the ocean nothing else aligned with what I saw within the chapel that day. It was then that I noticed the sailors aboard were now frantically running to and fro, securing ropes and adjusting sails as the captain shouted orders in a manner that was far from calm.

"What is happening?" yelled Bertrand to the captain as he strode past.

"We are caught in a current that is taking us off course. We will be back upon it soon," and with that he made way quickly to check upon his crew.

Bertrand shot me a glance but I looked away quickly so I would not have to acknowledge it. The snub itself sent a message very clearly though and he grunted before going to check on Aguinus.

The rough sea continued for another hour and as I kept looking ahead I saw some land come into view. I knew it could not be the Holy Lands just yet as they were hours away and we had not even passed the southernmost reaches of Italy.

The shore came closer and closer as the shouts of the captain grew louder and the sailors moved quicker. It was apparent to me and every other passenger upon that ship that they had no control of the vessel whatsoever.

"Well it looks as though we shall be visiting the Dalmatian Coast today," muttered a trader who stood nearby me.

I nodded but as I looked at the land that was quickly drawing close, I could see no port for us to land. Instead I saw cliffs and a jagged rocky shoreline. Within a breath I knew this would not end well and of course it did not.

The sound of the ship's wooden side hitting the rocks is something that I would never forget. It was not just the cracking of the wood, the screams of the people aboard or the sounds of the water rushing within the hull that would always remain with me. It was also the sensation that all I had believed in to bring me and my brothers to this moment had been false. The crashing of the boat and its reverberation hit my ears like a mocking laugh. The glares of my brothers once we were safe upon land were like a slap that stings beyond the momentary contact of the hand serving it.

I found a tree away from the water's edge and sat back against its trunk and began to take deep breaths. My heart was racing in a way I don't believe it had ever done before.

"This is the closest I have ever come to death," I thought and that in itself did little to slow my heart.

"Francis, what on earth do we do now?"

It was Bertrand standing over me and his tone matched the tense expression he was now offering me. However his words pulled me from the useless thought I was playing with and back to the present.

"Brother, I suggest we take a short spell to calm our bodies and minds. Then we can find lodgings to rest properly. I am sure we will find help to continue our passage," I replied though with some difficulty as my still fast breathing struggled to help me speak.

"Continue?" bellowed Bertrand. "For the love of all we do Francis, is this not enough of a sign that we should not continue?"

I opened my mouth to reply but Bertrand's hand flew up and he shook it at me.

"No! NO! You will not try and placate me with some sort of—of—sweetened reasoning that this is simply some hurdle we need to move past and then resume our plans. I will not stand here and accept that this is simply some evil that occurred to test or delay us. Nor will I ignore what I feel inside myself any longer.

Every one of us, EVERY one of us has had some feeling or sign that this journey was not to be and yet we all pushed those feelings aside and still made our way. We held our faith in you as it was your vision and you calmed us and made us believe our feelings were not true or of God. Well, my brother, I love and respect you with all my heart but today the Lord showed me that what is within me is far bigger and more important than any love or respect I can hold for something or someone outside of me.

I saw it in your eyes too Francis. Just before we boarded. Your eyes never hide the truth and today for the first time they showed me that you too had doubts.

You can continue on, but brother, it will be without me. My only journey from this place will be to return to Assisi—and—and if I am no longer welcome there, well then I will leave."

Bertrand's rant was spectacular and heartfelt. It was also the perfect length of time for me to have slowed my heart and breath, which allowed me to respond with two simple words.

"I agree."

"What?" Though it was the response he hoped for Bertrand was stunned.

"I agree. This did not feel right from the moment we decided to journey. I pushed aside this feeling and then, even worse, I counselled you all to do the same with your intuition.

Just because an action is based in devotion, goodwill and service does not make it whole or worthy of our time and energies. The timing can be wrong or its gifts may simply not be ready to be received.

Blind faith is not complete faith for it does not allow us a true relationship with God. I had forgotten this. God gifted us thoughts and feelings to serve us as well as him. I feel that this shipwreck was a very gentle way for him to remind me. I apologise for involving you all in this."

Bertrand put his hand upon his heart and nodded. "I apologise for speaking as such to you. I forgot my grace in addressing you."

Tears swelled in his eyes as he said this and despite the softness in which he now spoke I could not help but give a slight laugh.

"Oh my brother, it was perfect, as are you. I should hope none of you ever deny your emotions when you speak to me. We are all equals and you simply acted as such. In respecting your truth you will never disrespect me. In fact you honour me."

We took some time to find lodgings as we were far from any towns and the services they offered. While the other passengers settled to walk further or use the rowboat of the main ship to travel down the coast, we created a haven at the first farm we came upon.

We had only a minimal way to communicate with the farmer - great thanks to some small links between our language and that of the region

121

we had found ourselves in. Embellished with hand gestures and the gift of some gold we were able to be provided with a barn and a simple meal for the night.

As we settled back upon the hay and dimmed the lantern I heard Aguinus chuckle.

"It occurs to me that we could lie here and be resentful that our plans have been thwarted and that instead of arriving in the Holy Lands of Our Saviour as heroes we instead lie here amongst animals. However when I take that pause to connect with God I can see the gifts we have been offered. I see that the ship being stopped was a blessing. That we are spared and safe to continue our work as we pledged to God is all that matters," he said and though I could not see his face I knew he was smiling.

He continued. "When I first saw that vision in my dream of the ship crashing upon the rocks it seemed heavy and foreboding as it should have from the perspective of that moment in time. Now though, as I recall it from this moment, I see it as beautiful and encouraging."

We all paused for a moment and I felt each one of us take this in. I heard deep breaths and even a sigh. Then Bertrand spoke.

"Let us all pray I will never have to look back upon my vision of Francis' head upon a spike in such a way!"

CHAPTER NINETEEN

I set aside plans for travelling and missionary pursuits for some time. It was not with an air of loss by any means, but more an instinctive sense to reset my energies around the whole idea.

"Do you feel defeated?" I was asked upon my eventual return from the Dalmatian Coast.

"Defeat is not within my love of the Lord. This is merely a great reminder that the plans of men are but small details. While the love of the Lord and Our Saviour are alive in my heart then I conquer any distraction that life will present to me," I answered with a smile.

Thus I returned to my dedication and servitude of God where he deemed fit to have me placed. How could I have any remorse, regret or judgement upon the outcome of my decisions when the result was that I still had breath within my body to live my passion and serve the Lord and his teachings.

On my first morning back in Assisi I prayed for guidance.

"Lord, you showed how I was not ready, but I hunger to make my service more than it is. Show me how I can do this?"

I breathed in silence for several minutes and felt the sun through the windows of the small chapel begin to heat the room around me. Then some clouds came over closing off the warm light and the room dropped temperature suddenly.

I opened my eyes, rose from my knees and made way to prepare for mass. I knew in my heart God would always show me the way.

It was several days later at the Sunday morning mass that I noticed a new group of people within the congregation. It was not rare for people to travel from afar to attend our church so new faces were common and most often they would blend in. Today though, they did not.

They came dressed in noble refinery: this would also not have garnered any attention, as many nobles came to satisfy their curiosity. It was the size of the group that did so. There were at least twenty of them of all ages and both sexes. They walked into the church as one unit making heads turn which they seemed to enjoy.

At the front was a man who was clearly the figurehead. He decided where they would sit and who was placed beside him. When the mass was over he remained within his seat and frantically waved to get my attention as I stood watching the congregation leave.

I nodded to acknowledge him but this clearly was not enough. He then beckoned me with just as much enthusiasm and what I imagine he believed his authority to do so. Unperturbed I made my way to him.

"Good morning," I said as I came close. "God be with you."

"And also with you," he responded as he pushed at those sitting beside him. "Get up! Get up! Make way for the monsignor!" he snapped at them.

"My friend, I am no monsignor and I have no time to sit on this day. I will stand," I replied calmly.

"Oh," he responded somewhat flatly. "You know I have travelled a fair distance to hear you preach."

The word "preach" clawed at me as these days I far more preferred the word "teach" but I smiled and resisted the urge to correct him yet again.

"We are honoured you would do so to hear the word of the Lord," I said and bowed my head.

Thankfully we had satisfied all he had come to see and hear. Perhaps even more so than he had hoped. He looked about our church and our community and he sensed the truth of what we were doing.

The man snapped his fingers to another of the men in his group still sitting close by and this other man reached into his sleeve and pulled out a purse filled with coins.

"I wish to support you," my new friend said to me as he handed me the money.

"I thank you most humbly. Such donations do much to further our work and allow relief to the truly needy who we serve," I said with all sincerity.

The man stood now and straightened his coat. He extended his hand to shake mine.

"Francis, I am Count Orlando di Chiusi and I hope that we can continue to help one another."

The Count returned the following week and the one after as well until his presence was as common as any others. Sometimes his companions would number many, other times there would be but a handful.

"They come as they choose. I cannot force devotion upon them," he explained to another parishioner when asked about this.

Each week we would speak though no longer would I be summoned to his pew. Instead he would make his way to find me either at the altar or outside in the monastery gardens.

I came to enjoy our weekly conversations and each week he showed a growing love of the Lord and his teachings. Often he would tell me how something within the Sunday mass would reveal its truth to him during the week, inspiring him to pray and give more of his love to God.

"It was amazing. Your brother spoke of compassion for our neighbours and not just our family. This week several of the farmers within my lands fell ill and could not attend to pay taxes as they should. In the past I would have not hesitated to punish or fine them as I am entitled, but instead I felt their suffering. I sent food and medicines for them. Within days they were upon my door to pay their taxes and express their thanks and gratitude.

One even said to me that they felt the love of God in what I did and that alone cured him. While another said my patience and understanding lifted his concerns and stress, allowing him the relief to recover in peace.

If I had exerted my authority with no feeling it would have made my situation worse. These men would have worried and become more ill. They would have been even later in their payments and suffered worse fines.

Instead I set aside my pride and vanity. In doing so I allowed the love of God to serve us all."

Despite my hatred at the injustice of the feudal tax system I nodded and smiled. That a man of such standing could allow compassion within this system in any way was a miracle of our time. I could never be ungrateful for such a thing.

One day Orlando ended our conversation with an invitation.

"You must come to my home some day. It is not so far as I make it to be," he laughed when he admitted this. "You would be there within an hour or so upon a carriage."

I had become so used to refusing such offers these days that I shook my head immediately. Visits that were not essentially of my work were just distractions and my order was bigger; I could not leave for anything so trivial as to call on a parishioner for social means alone.

The Count would not accept this. "Please! This is not just to enjoy food and wine. I—I—there is something I wish to share with you," he almost begged.

As I looked into his eyes I could see this was indeed not just a frivolous invitation. I stopped shaking my head and paused.

"Thank you my friend. I will indeed accept," I responded with that sense of trust that is so deep you cannot question it.

"Wonderful. Then my prayers for this are answered. I knew the

Lord would not let you say no. Well, not a second time anyway."

Orlando sent a carriage for me and three other brothers to take us to his estate. It was a grand carriage that seemed to oppose all that we stood for. When I came to climb upon it I saw the looks upon the other monk's faces and sighed deeply.

"Why are we not walking?" Rufino asked bluntly.

"So as to save time and make haste our return," I offered.

"We have walked further with no concerns for time," he retorted.

"And that was when our order and its demands were much different," I responded. "There is no sin in accepting a carriage ride to make good of our time and services, despite its ornamentation."

Rufino raised one eyebrow. "Well then I can tolerate the misuse of gold upon its woodwork for such a rationale."

We rode in silence. It somehow seemed that to sing as we usually did would make the irony of riding in such a vehicle even more ridiculous. Rufino took out the cushion from below him and set it aside as though denying himself that comfort would make himself feel better about his part in this. Within thirty minutes he returned it to beneath him making me laugh.

"It appears all our walking may have strengthened your feet and legs at the expense of making other parts more delicate," I joked and we all broke into laughter.

The Count's estate was magnificent. We rode through farmlands that were lush and well tended. The lands were placed to the base of the Apennines and were watered with the continual melting of snow in springtime leaving them prepared for the hot summers and then the cold of the other seasons.

I looked up to the mountains and saw them as protective and yet unforgiving as though they could nurture in one moment and turn on you the next. They were both a mother with gentle love and a father with strict discipline. I fell in love with them in that moment and it would be a love and respect that would never die.

I knew they had called me here. Orlando had provided a human invitation but he had been the instrument created by God to do so.

It is fascinating when a land or region calls to us. I know when somewhere called to me it was always of God's choosing and to provide me with an opportunity to connect more so with his teaching. Looking

126

up to the mountains I knew another of these opportunities was about to unfold. All I had to do was be willing for this, and allow it to happen.

Orlando's house staff greeted us and showed us into his large home where he was waiting to receive us with the most sincere and earnest of grins. We were made to rest and eat, all while he spoke over and over of the privilege of having us within his home. Then we offered to lead some prayers.

"Might you have somewhere suitable?" I asked and the grin upon his face grew even larger.

Orlando led us outside and across a great lawn that was edged in immaculately trimmed hedges and trees. He walked briskly as though he could not get us to where he wanted fast enough so that we almost had to run to keep up with him.

At the opposite edge of the garden the hedge had an opening, framed on either side by a pillar topped with an urn holding a small shrub. We stepped through and Orlando kept to the side, his chest heaving at having moved so quickly. He had not caught his breath so could not speak clearly just yet and instead simply raised his arm and held his hand out for us to look where it was pointed.

There before us was a chapel sitting within the clearing of a small forest. It was neither small nor grand but it was significantly more than a token construction in which to worship. I recalled my dilapidated church in which I began and smiled. By this time Orlando had caught his breath.

"I built this for my family. We used to have prayer in the parlour but I felt we needed a dedicated space for such things. I sometimes invite others... and maybe someday we could have a Franciscan brother live here to preach to our community?"

I shuddered once more at the word "preach" but set that aside to take in the beauty of what Orlando had created. We walked inside and I saw that despite its small size no attention to detail had been spared. This was as carefully thought out as any church in any village.

"Who leads your prayers?" asked our brother Leo.

"Oh—um—most days I do," he replied and I saw his cheeks turn slightly red.

"Well that would be the duty of the patriarch in the absence of a priest," I offered and looked away as I did not wish to further his blushing. "Rufino, would you mind doing the honours today?"

We prayed for an hour when I noticed that Orlando was growing restless.

"I fear we have carried on too long for you. We should surely make to return to Assisi," I suggested but Orlando shook his head fervently.

"No you mustn't go yet. I just—I just need to show you something more and we must make way before the sun drops too low in the sky," he explained.

Once more at the front of the chapel, we now made way to circle around it until we were at the very back of the building. Orlando then led us away through the trees.

There was a rough track that we walked upon letting us know this was not something new we were about to see. Orlando walked sure-foot-edly indicating this also. We were soon at the base of one of the mountains and it soared above us.

"La Verna!" Orlando exclaimed.

"She is magnificent," I said in awe.

"She is glorious," Orlando shouted out to the mountain as though he wanted her to know.

We all looked about and wondered what we had been brought here for. There were no more buildings, be they for worship or otherwise. All that there was to be seen apart from grasses and trees was the continuation of the trail that led up the side of the mountain.

"Come, come," said Orlando and beckoned me in much the same way he did when he first came to my church.

We were then led up the mountainside. Not so far thankfully and we were standing upon a level area. Even though it was high above the ground from where we started, it was so dense with trees to the side that we could not look down. It was like a small haven and we all smiled as we stood within it.

"This is beautiful," I said softly. "It is like a chapel in its own way."

"Yes, yes, but look here," Orlando waved his hand furiously once more and walked towards the slope of the mountain opposite the trees. I could see now an opening that looked like the rocky wall had been split open. Orlando stepped aside and allowed me to now walk into the crevice.

There was little light once I was between the rocks and my eyes played with this until I could make out within the shadows that this was a small cave. It was large enough for perhaps two men at best to stand in with reasonable room or for one man to sit and not feel crowded.

I stepped completely into the cave and now that I no longer blocked the entrance some more light came in and I could see the walls were smooth as though the space had been worked upon. The floor was likewise and clear of any debris.

Orlando remained outside but spoke so I could hear him. "It was much smaller when I found it. I am still not sure what led me here... well of course I am. It was God! I have heard of many great channels of God taking such retreats in solitude in such places to allow their wisdom to come through.

As soon as I saw it I knew it was the perfect location for retreat. It gathers the sun for some warmth but is protected. It was just too small so I had some men make it bigger for me."

"Who has used it thus far?" asked Morico.

"Oh—ah—just me for prayer," Orlando answered sheepishly and I imagined his face was bright red as he did so.

I also knew he had wanted to hear the voice of God in the way he imagined the great prophets had. From the wear of the trail up here he had been doing that for some time. I also imagined that he never spent more than a few hours here; returning to the comfort of his home just a short walk away when his body and mind grew weary.

As I stood there I was almost back within my prison cell, with that small shard of light coming to me from the tiny window in the door. This cave was even smaller and yet with no door the sense of the outside with its smells and sounds free to enter made it seem bigger. I walked back outside and shielded my eyes until they adjusted to the light once more.

"I want to gift this to you," the words seemed to almost explode from Orlando's mouth. And in that moment, I realised this had been the intention of his invitation all along.

CHAPTER TWENTY

Orlando had indeed been holding his own retreats in the cave for well over a year. He had felt a calling to converse with God that he believed was born of the same inspiration of the great prophets that he read about in the bible. That calling led him to build the chapel and he began to lead prayers for his family hoping it would show God that he was worthy.

When the family were done, he would kneel alone before the altar and pray more though it would actually seem more like begging. One day as he made his way to the chapel he happened to look up at the nearby mountain and smiled as he recalled the story of Moses alone upon Mount Sinai writing the commandments.

As he remembered this something within him was struck as though by lightning and instead of going into the chapel Orlando began to climb the mountainside.

"Of course," he laughed to himself. "All this time in my chapel and I should have been upon the mountain as all the prophets did."

He climbed with such fervour that he had to stop soon to catch his breath. That was where he found the cave and its somewhat fortuitous appearance as he gathered himself was seen as a sign that this was the place to commune with God. So he did indeed bring two men to work upon it and within a week it was far more suitable to his perceived needs.

He would sit for hours, praying to be shown some wisdom. Then as the sun set and the cave cooled he would drag his feet back home for a warm meal and the comfort of his bed.

Sometimes days and even weeks would pass that he could not even come to the cave. Such is the life of a count with an estate and lands to gather taxes from. Also there were times when his wife could no longer tolerate such behaviour.

"I cannot lie for you anymore. People come calling to visit and I say you are out checking on the lands but they do not see you about. How can I say, 'oh my husband sits in a cave for some godforsaken belief he can turn into Moses?'"

He would stop for some time and his wife would be placated that he could act as normal as she believed he needed to be but soon something inside would call him again. Once more he would sit for hours and he would hear nothing.

Then one day as the sun dropped and the shadows of the trees closed off the little light he had, Orlando called out loud with all the voice he could muster.

"If this is not meant to be, if I am not worthy of your audience then let me know how I can serve you? I know with all my heart I was meant to find this place. I believe with every part of the very soul you gifted me with that this place is meant for some greatness to serve you. Show me what it is that you want to become of this."

With that Orlando stood and left the cave for the last time. Now his wife had to contend with his brooding and a constant scowl on his face.

"Maybe you should return to your cave so I don't have to endure this sullen demeanour. It is like being at a continual funeral," she scoffed one evening over dinner.

Orlando did not even have the energy to make a retort and put her back in her place as he knew he should. Instead he ate as though she said nothing.

"We must attend a ball on Friday at the Della Monte estate. You do remember?" she jabbed at him.

Orlando grunted and nodded to reply. His wife sighed and put down her fork.

"Can I ask of you—can I beg of you to act as though you are slightly interested in the event once we get there?"

Orlando kept eating but answered quite civilly. "Yes my dear. I promise to attend and act out the most perfect count, husband and whatever else is required to suit the occasion."

His wife did not respond but Orlando heard her whimper and push her chair back to leave. As she got to the doorway she stopped and turned to him.

"You know I do understand. It's just that I don't see the point of being so morbid about it. You aren't the first to NOT be chosen. You won't be the last either. Please accept that God has other plans for you."

Orlando slammed his fork down making his wife scurry before he could spit any nasty words at her.

"How could you understand?" he screamed behind her anyway. Servants came in and began to clear the table so Orlando cut short the rest of the tirade he was going to unleash.

How could anyone understand the pain of feeling something so strongly within yourself and then not having that come to any sort of fruition? He now had an empty chapel and a barren cave sitting as some sort of sick symbols of his failure to fill himself with God's messages. They should have become pilgrimage sites but now they were just permanent reminders of how he had failed.

So Orlando tried to return to the life of a normal noble but the ache from his heart burned still. He donned his finery and rode in the carriage with his wife to the party that week, making his best attempt to smile lest he ruin her night. She loved these balls and he truly did not want to spoil it for her.

When they arrived he was soon separated from her. She made way to join the women sitting upon couches to one end of the room while the men gathered to smoke and drink at the other end. The two genders only mixing to dance and this was the younger ones mostly anyway.

So as his wife floated away and the young people bobbed, swayed and spun across the ballroom floor he squared his shoulders and prepared himself for the small talk and posturing he would now be part of with the men.

"Ah Orlando, so good to see your face. You have been a scarce sight these past months. I hope you have not been ill?" asked the host Count Angelo Della Monte.

Orlando beamed the smile he had been practising. "No, not at all. You know how our estates just take so much time."

"Oh yes, yes, yes," Angelo then leaned in close. "Not to mention keeping these wives happy."

With that he leant back and roared with laughter as Orlando pretended to be likewise amused. Inside he gave thanks the music was loud enough to dull Angelo's laugh. Angelo turned to another man who was standing beside him.

"Orlando, this is Lord Benedict of the Scarlini family."

"I know you," Orlando said.

"Yes you do. I visited with you many times as a child," Benedict replied.

"He won't be visiting again though will you?" yelled Angelo as he grabbed roughly at the young man's shoulder. "This man is going to become a monk with that new order in Assisi."

Orlando and Benedict's eyes locked in mutual embarrassment at Angelo's behaviour but within a second it shifted and the ache deep within Orlando's heart became a fire once more.

"Won't you tell me more about this please," Orlando did all he could to not actually beg the information from him. He knew with every fibre of his being that Benedict was going to show him what God intended of the chapel and cave.

Angelo fell away, busy with his hosting duties and the two spoke without interruption. Benedict shared his calling to come and hear our mass and the immediate decision to join us. They sat and talked until the music stopped and Orlando's wife came looking for him.

133

"I am just saying my final farewells and doing some last duties to make my family happy. They deserve that respect for all they have done for me," Benedict explained.

As Benedict spoke, with each anecdote and insight he shared, Orlando felt his calling open and expand. Then he shared what he had been through.

"You must go to Assisi!" Benedict's eyes lit up. "Talk to Francis and the others. I am sure they will guide you."

So Orlando made his way to our church but did not know how to begin to even tell me. He brought others who were curious after Benedict spoke so much of joining us during his farewells. They in turn made it difficult for us to speak and that is why some weeks he came with so few as well, in order to make it easier to interact with me.

Eventually he decided that if he could somehow get me to his home, the sight of the chapel and then the cave would speak for themselves. So when he announced that the cave was a gift to me it was no wonder that I could feel this was more than just a simple exchange or offering of some property. This was indeed a plan laid out by God. Unfortunately along the way it had made use of Orlando in what seemed to be a somewhat cruel detour.

He explained all this as we stood upon the mountainside. Each one of us remained silent as he spoke and felt the pain he had been through. Yet our hearts swelled as we felt his dedication and devotion.

"Sir, you are an inspiration," whispered Leo and Orlando's eyes filled with tears.

"Please say you will accept this gift," he said to me so gently.

I nodded. "But of course I do."

It was a simple agreement that would have far-reaching outcomes. Orlando's vision of this becoming a pilgrimage site would one day come true.

I began with short visits. Just a few days at a time. The solitude and silence were quite frankly a relief from the constant activities of our community. To even withdraw into a quiet room or the small morning chapel were no comparison. Sitting with the knowledge that on the other side of the door were your duties and commitments is very different to the solidity of a mountain and a curtain of trees, while you pray high above the ordinary world.

Across my lifetimes I speak often of moments of such solitude and how such retreats allow an expansion of inner wisdom and peace. They were invaluable parts of my lifetimes whose benefits and rewards were above any measure.

When I first took retreat within La Verna I imagined it would be something akin to my time in prison. On that first day I immediately knew it would not be.

Orlando walked with me to the base of the mountain that day and shook my hand. Then he gestured to the mountain. "May the Lord be with you."

I nodded to accept his blessing.

"And also with you." I returned his blessing as I ought.

Then I made my way around his chapel and began upon the path that would take me to the cave. As I did so I recalled how I had been taken to my prison cell. I had not walked freely; I was bound and dragged so that my feet were barely able to walk as they should. I was pushed into the cold cell and shackled to the bolt in the floor. Then the door was closed and I heard the latch slide and the key turn within its lock. All I had with me was my heartbeat, my breath and that small square of light in the door that reminded me there was a world outside.

Today I walked freely. This was my choice. I looked up and saw some birds circling above me in the sky. I heard others sing within the trees around me.

Freedom.

Every beat of their wings. Every note of their song. The birds reminded me that I was as free as they were. I had shed the past of my family. I had shed the rules of a church that had lost its way. I held no plans for what was to come as I had handed that to my faith and trust in the Lord. I was free.

This is why I connected so with the birds and they are my symbol. I understood their freedom as I embodied mine. All animals are in the moment. They do not dwell upon a past. They live to embrace life as best they can. Yes, that can amount to simple survival, but without the weight of a story they are free to be their essence.

I looked back up to the birds circling above me and smiled. Soon I would be within the cave and no longer would I enjoy this sight. I would once again though when my retreat was complete. In the meantime I thanked God for his creation and the blessing of my freedom.

Yes, once more I would be within a truly quiet place. It was no longer a prison nor was it a test for I was not a captive or a student anymore. I walked upon La Verna to the small womb she offered me and I did so free and as the master of my life.

CHAPTER TWENTY-ONE

The call of distant lands was soon upon me once more. Now I looked to places even more challenging than the Holy Lands of Jerusalem and its surrounds. It just did not seem fitting that I travel there. Actually it was not so much that I did not feel to go there, but that other lands called to me.

My time within the mountain cave had cleared much about how I felt about travelling and taking our teachings elsewhere. It had not come to me in a vision while I prayed there. There were no voices that spoke to me and told me where to be. Instead I dreamed of where I should go.

The dreams began in such a way that at first I did not pay much attention. My truly prophetic dreams had always been so literal that they made way to my awareness without fuss or symbolism. I did so enjoy such direct communications. Allegories, fables and metaphors always seemed a waste of energy to me. I could never understand why a man or woman would choose such an indirect way to receive a message.

The first dream as such saw me stand within a strange land. I looked about and could sense it was a place of extreme heat. The people were clothed in elaborate robes to shield themselves from the harsh sunlight but I saw glimpses of hands and faces that showed dark skin. Very dark skin. More so than that of the Spaniards or even our fishermen and farmers of the south.

Beyond the scenery and the colour of their skin I could also sense an emptiness. I felt beliefs that were ages old, as were ours, and while there was respect and reverence I could sense a disconnection from these beliefs. It was just as I had felt with our church and the people here in Italy. The dream returned over several nights. The details might change slightly but the sense was the same.

It instilled within me a new fervour for my work with God. So many religions had survived for so long but now seemed to be followed by people with empty rituals and had become more like social constructs to regulate people rather than imbue within them a deep connection to the creator who had designed our very existence.

Then our Lord had gifted us with a grand teacher to show us a new way to love and be loved within the comfort of the Holy Father's embrace. I did not see other religions as wrong or outdated. I just saw people who were missing out on the beauty and grace of knowing Our Saviour. It is only natural when you have allowed such love within your life and witnessed the blessings it has given you and others that one would want more to know of this also.

Please know that I never spoke of any other religions as infidels, heathens, blasphemers or otherwise. These are terms used by the weak, the manipulative, the ignorant and those seeking power over others. My view of our mission work was always to reconnect people to the truth of God and the joy of Jesus' teachings. After all how could spreading the message of love, compassion and redemption be anything but a gift to humanity?

So once more I set sail for distant lands and just as I knew it was a different person who walked to my cave, I too knew it was a different person who would now set sail. To make this even clearer I aimed in the opposite direction. This time I would make way to Morocco.

I set sail from the east coast this time to wind across the northern shores of Africa. It should have been daunting to head to a land entrenched in the teachings of Islam for generation after generation. Its royalty as devoted to the religion as its people, believing that one of the duties of their rule was to uphold the holy word of the Koran and the way of life it prescribed.

However it did not have the history of the Holy Lands. I would not be seen as another militant campaigner trying to continue the conflicts of the past. This was a land that could possibly have fresh eyes, ears and, most importantly, hearts for our teaching. I stood upon the deck of the ship and looked forward with the utmost confidence.

Italy vanished upon the horizon behind us and the coast of Africa appeared to the south. Then something within my stomach turned making me grab at it. I tried to straighten but couldn't and reached for a railing to steady myself.

I tried to convince myself that I was seasick but I knew it was not. That affliction was not one I was prone to and besides this was entirely different to that which I could see about me in the ones with pale faces who retched continually over the side of the ship. This was harsher and more acute.

Leo, one of the few brothers I allowed with me, saw me stumble as I grabbed for support and ran to my side.

"Francis, what is it?" he cried.

"I—I don't know," was all I could respond before I collapsed upon the deck and fell into unconsciousness.

When I awoke there was a strange face above me looking down through spectacles.

"Mmm..." he mumbled as he seemed to search my eyes for some sign. Then he spoke in a Spanish dialect. I was too weak to even be able to hear what he said and fell back to sleep.

It was several days later when I opened my eyes again. The spectacled man was gone and I heard someone move nearby.

"Who is there?" I called out.

"It is me, Rufino," came the reply. "Leo sent for us as soon as you landed."

"Oh Rufino," I had tears of relief to hear his voice. "What happened? Where am I?"

"My brother, I can tell you that you are in Spain. As for what happened? Well, no doctor can tell us so that will remain a mystery. I imagine you remember collapsing upon the boat?" I nodded and Rufino continued. "The others requested the ship bring you to Spain. They felt, rightly so, that you would be safer here, and well the language would be easier."

"How long?" I asked.

"It has been almost two weeks now. Though at times you cried out in pain, you mostly slept. The past few days the cries have been less and your fever has declined."

"Take me home. Please."

"Soon, Francis. Soon," Rufino replied.

With that I began to cry.

Was I never meant to take my teachings to other lands? Had I insulted God by taking the teachings of Jesus to a land so devoted to Islam? I heard a resounding "no" to each of these questions.

Why had my body failed me so? I could not blame any other for such an occurrence. There was no negligent crew or weather anomaly to cause a wreck. I had not ignored any feeling within me.

All I knew in that moment was that I needed to return to Assisi. My energy was needed in the lands of Italy and within the community I had created. Others could do our mission work. That is what my trust in myself showed me in that moment with such clarity - it was the truth that our teachings should be elsewhere. It just did not have to be me.

On my return I asked of my brothers who would be willing to do such work in these lands. Five men stepped forward immediately; Berard, Peter, Otho, Accursius, and Adjutus. Most of them were new but this did not diminish their capabilities. In fact it was as though this made them all the more appropriate. Not set in any ways of monastic routine in Assisi it seemed they would be freer to adapt to any challenges they might face.

Adjutus was the only one who showed any doubts once he asked to join the mission. "I just fear I do not know the bible verses so well. My memory is not always the best for recitations," he confessed to me.

"Then do not recite. Jesus would not wish you to simply be someone to repeat his words. Do you understand and feel the depth of his teachings?"

"Yes."

"Do you not carry a passion within your heart to share these teachings and guide people to the love of Our Lord and Our Saviour?"

"With all my heart and soul."

"Then share from your heart and your soul. They will forget the words as easily as you do, even more so. What they will carry with them will be the love and truth within what you speak."

A week after they left Italy we received word that the men had disembarked in Spain and while this was not as planned I felt it was no detriment to their duties. In fact it was perfect as southern Spain at this time was well dominated by the teachings of Islam. I smiled broadly as I imagined them there.

Berard had chosen perfectly. Once aboard the ship the other four men's doubts found voices and were spoken. Berard listened with compassion and nodded. He understood the hesitation to go to a new land immersed in another religion and with a strange language. His knowledge of the local language had tempered such thoughts within him and he knew this was a personal advantage which offered him a solace that the others did not have.

It was Berard who decided they would land in Spain where there was a significant Muslim population. Once there he acted like a mentor, guiding the others with not just his knowledge of the Moroccan dialect but also with his rudimentary understanding of Islam. Within a few weeks the others were clearer and more confident with what would lie ahead across the strait.

Months later when news of their beheadings at the hand of the Moroccan king reached us, the emotions we felt were mixed. There was remorse from those of us that had agreed to the mission at all. There was grief at the loss of our brothers. There were waves of relief from those who had not chosen to go.

Such emotions are small and so human. We allow them as they are part of our conditioning and essential to who we are and how we connect with one another. When one is in service to the Lord though, such emotions must come back into balance within the grand scheme of what one is achieving.

Not for one moment did I wish any missionary to come to such demise, and especially not in such a brutal way. I heard that they were threatened over and over again and then upon their imprisonment they were beaten and tortured. Yet not one man faltered in their faith and commitment to Christ.

Even when the head of Otho was cut first and his blood pooled before them, they did not flinch or beg for mercy. Instead they remained defiant and strong, because the faith and love they had in their hearts would mean no matter the fate of their body, their spirit would be carried by God.

Yes we could have just mourned their deaths, but there was something quite majestic in their passage to heaven. Even more importantly we had to celebrate their unyielding passion to serve and honour their beliefs. We could not see them as victims of the king's scimitar. We chose to celebrate them as victors of their own love and that of God.

Our first martyrs would not be our last, but they would be the grandest for they showed to us all, as well as the world around us, the depths of our dedication and service.

It would have been easy to also deduce my illness on the way to Morocco as God's way to save my own life that I would continue to lead my order. Indeed this became something that was spoken of often and freely. Sometimes it would amuse me to hear such things and other times it would actually bring up some ire within me.

It was not the manner in which it was spoken nor the person who spoke it that would bring out either reaction. It was the battle within myself to still make sense of my collapse and its timing. Sometimes I saw it as a blessing, but other times I saw it as some weakness within me that had not allowed my own martyrdom.

I prayed and prayed over this but received no answer. That in itself had to become the response I would accept. Within this acceptance I had to let go of any story I wished to hold around my seeming failure to arrive in Morocco. The story became simply that I fell ill and returned home.

It becomes so easy to want to see some significance in everything. To make it a failure or a success; to understand why circumstances do not go as planned. When we surrender into acceptance we simply agree to God's plan, and he need never explain himself to any man. Not even a true servant such as myself.

No, I would not question this anymore. I would accept the plans of a creator who I loved beyond measure and trusted with my entire heart.

CHAPTER TWENTY-TWO

Our order continued to grow and spread across Italy and to other countries in Europe. Elias went to Jerusalem and began a new chapter there that still continues its work in the Holy Land in your modern day. My dealings with Rome continued and we were granted a "protector" due to our martyrs.

All in all we were a substantial and noted presence and body within the Catholic Church. Our teachings were considered exemplary and the men of our brotherhood were known to be as educated and wise as they were dedicated. What we sometimes lacked in our administrative skills we made up for with our integrity to serve Our Lord.

I travelled the length of Italy to visit all the orders we had established. I prayed and taught with our brothers. I reminded them of why we had begun our own brotherhood and when I returned to Assisi I felt renewed and refreshed in my faith for the men who had chosen to join us.

Back in Assisi I received a guest soon after my return. He was a young Crusader, fresh back from Egypt. He arrived at the monastery, his skin dark from the African sun and his eyes bright from the adventure he had been upon.

"To ride for Our Lord and show the truth of Our Saviour is a wonderful tonic to take into battle," he smiled widely as he said this and I pictured him upon his horse with his sword drawn and ready. Somehow this did not seem to inspire anything within me.

I wanted to ask him how it felt to watch those of a different faith be slaughtered for the same God as that they went to defend? I wanted to ask him how proud did he imagine Jesus to be, having blood spilt in his name. I wanted to ask so many things but I smiled politely and asked something else.

"Will you miss your sword when you are here?"

The young man faltered as I asked this. "But—surely—I would be free to return across the sea as your mission within the Crusades?"

I shook my head. "No you would not. You choose the way of our brotherhood which is without weapons or battles."

He looked down and I could see there was a struggle in his mind. I continued on.

"There will be no more armour. No more gold. No more plans, strategies or tactics. There are no generals or commanders. Here we just have elders who have served longer and know the gospel a bit more thoroughly. There are no superiors, no subservient beings. All we have here is our faith and devotion, along with our passion to teach and share the Lord's work."

"And those robes..." he whimpered and I nodded. Then he looked to our tonsured scalps. "I suppose that is part of it too?"

I nodded once more and within an hour our young Christian soldier was making his way on the road out of Assisi.

I did not wish to see him as the general example of what a Crusader was but for the most part it was the truth. The Crusaders were fuelled by adrenaline and glory and not at all by the true rewards of teaching Jesus' words. For if one was truly connected to the gospel they would never even consider using war to spread its truth.

The Crusaders were men who were bought to fight for those wanting more power. They were pawns of politicians, inspired by the human rewards promised to them by wealthy men. They could not have been further from the truth of Our Saviour.

In 1219 it is recorded that I made way to Egypt, which I did with one companion, our brother Eduardo. It is said that I did this in order to convert the Sultan, and in honesty I would have truly loved to have done this, but the truth of my journey was so that I could show there was a better, more graceful way to share the word of Jesus. The only people I truly wanted or even hoped to convert were the Crusaders.

I arrived during a massive siege of Damietta, a large city at the mouth of the Nile River, just inland from the coast. Damietta had long been considered to be the key to capturing and controlling Egypt. At this time there was fierce fighting from both sides with neither making any progress.

Eduardo and I found lodgings well back from the fighting with no intention to be close. I looked at the city from the open rooftop of my guesthouse. We could see the white and blue of the Crusaders uniforms and tents circling the city. I could hear the battle cries and hear the whoosh of another volley of arrows followed by the inevitable screams and groans of the wounded.

"So senseless," I muttered out loud.

"How is this God's work?" spat Eduardo.

"It isn't," I replied. "How can it be to set your children upon each other?"

For that is what we all were. The Muslims within the city were no less children of God and called upon his love and protection just as those outside the city walls did with their embroidered crosses upon their chests. I sighed, closed my eyes and began to pray.

I felt Jesus come and stand beside me. I did not open my eyes. I did not need to see him. I apologised to him.

"Lord forgive them. They have lost their way," I asked of him.

Jesus put his hand gently upon my shoulder.

"My brother, they have not lost their way. They are men choosing the way of men. Remember the way you have chosen. That is all you need to worry about."

I opened my eyes and looked back at the siege. From a distance you could admire the formation of the Christians outside, organised into phalanxes with each man in his perfect place. I looked upon the city and saw how the battlements had been designed to make sure every inch of land that edged to its walls could be monitored and defended.

It was all a perfect design, playing out just as the generals and architects had planned. Within this tableau, each man played the perfect role. It was brutal and yet beautiful in its own way.

Within a week of my arrival it was clear that neither party was making progress. A message was sent from the Sultan to the leader of the Crusaders:

"Surrender now and return to your lands! Remain and die. We have resources to continue and will never relinquish our home to you."

The Crusader's general let the message fall from his hand on the floor. He rubbed at his eyes which had not known sleep in any constructive way for over a month now. The constant state of battle was beginning to take its toll both physically and emotionally.

Oh how he wanted to surrender. He just wanted to sleep so much. The General wanted a meal at his family table, then to make love to his wife and wake with her beside him. He wanted to collapse upon the floor right where he was and never wake up. He just wanted this to be over.

He could never surrender. All he could do would be withdraw and return to Europe, but to even do that now, with his men as exhausted as he was, would leave them open to attacks anyway. He slumped forward as his officers looked upon him waiting for his response so they could write it down for the messenger.

"Sir... Sir... what shall we say?"

The General sat straight in his chair and looked about him.

"We will not surrender or withdraw. I will request a ceasefire that we may negotiate to claim Damietta."

One of the officers sighed deeply and loudly enough for the General to hear and know of his disapproval. The General turned to him, his eyes red and glassy.

"You do not approve?"

"No, not at all. That would have to be one of the weakest plans I have ever heard," sneered the man.

Suddenly the General did not feel so tired. He stood from his chair and walked to the Officer, standing so close that their noses almost touched and they could smell the stench of each other's unbathed bodies.

"You will carry the message to the Sultan yourself and if he doesn't accept, feel free to make a better offer."

The Officer turned pale. In the past the Sultan responded to the Crusader's demands and offers by sending his rejection back attached to the severed head of the messenger. There would be no chance to make a better offer and both of the men knew this.

So the Officer, with scroll in his hand, walked tentatively to the main gate of Damietta, under the protection of shields and the hoisting of a white flag to signal that a message was being conveyed. All the men he passed carried the same expression of knowing just what his fate would be.

They opened a small door within the gate to let him pass, on his own with no escort and the Officer thought he might faint as they checked him for weapons. He was then led to meet with the Sultan.

He was stopped again by more guards, dressed more elaborately and he realised these were the personal guards of the Sultan. They muttered angrily at the ones already accompanying the man and these first guards moved aside so the new guards could once again check the Officer for weapons which they did far more thoroughly. The Officer sighed. His fear now turned to anger and grew even more as he was grabbed by the upper arm and pushed onwards.

By the time he was standing before the Sultan he began to pray for his death to come quickly so this ridiculous scene would be over as soon as possible. Beside the Sultan stood an interpreter who read the message, then read it again to be sure of the words before he leant down and whispered in the Sultan's ear. All the while the Sultan kept his eye upon the Officer. As the translator spoke softly to him the Sultan began to smile.

"So, they send someone important with the message this time?" he smirked as the translator repeated this for the Officer.

"Yes. Our General wants you to know how serious he considers this offer," came the reply from the stony-faced Officer.

"A serious offer requires a serious reply."

With that the Sultan motioned for the interpreter to lean close and quietly relayed just what his answer would be. The interpreter stepped to the side where there was a table with some parchment and ink and he began to write out what had been said to him. To the Officer this felt like an eternity and he watched him intently. Not least so that he could break eye contact with the Sultan whose deep green eyes seemed to burn into him.

He also knew that the completion of the message would now require its means of transport be prepared. So as the interpreter placed his quill back into its pot and threw dust upon the writing to blot the wet ink, he took a deep breath and it suddenly felt as though the room was spinning.

The Sultan burst out laughing and said something loudly. As the interpreter rolled up the parchment he smiled.

"He says he has never seen anyone as pale as you - and he has met someone from China!"

The interpreter handed the scroll to the Officer and turned to bow to the Sultan who spoke again. The interpreter turned back to the Officer.

"You are free to go."

All that happened next was a blur for the Officer. He thought he bowed to the Sultan and thanked him but if you asked him this later he would tell that he had no memory of it at all. All he could recall was walking back down along a corridor with two guards, wondering which door would take him to his death.

When they emerged from the building into a courtyard he saw the wooden block with the axe next to it and it was as though all his blood emptied from his body. Within his thoughts he began to recite the Our Father prayer, but the guards walked him past the block so that they were soon out of the courtyard and back before the very gate through which he had entered. They opened the small doorway once more and pushed him through so that he landed upon his face, spread eagled upon the ground outside, the scroll grasped in his right hand.

The dirt had never tasted better. If it weren't that he would have to walk back through all the men the Officer would have cried with relief. Instead he stood himself up and without so much as dusting his hands, he straightened his shoulders and began to march.

As he came to the first men he called out loudly, "Our Father, who art in heaven..." and the men joined in the prayer. Every man he passed joined in and they said it as loud as they could. When the prayer was finished but he was yet to arrive at the General's tent they all began the prayer over again.

It was not just the men that flanked his walk who prayed out loud. The prayer rippled out around him so that every Crusader around the city spoke the words. Within the city walls the Sultan could hear them.

"They call their men to prayer. Let us call ours!"

"But Sire it is not time yet," said one of his ministers.

"Do you think Allah cares for what time it is if we want to pray?" he snapped back.

Within minutes the Egyptians were crying out their Islamic prayers to match the Christians outside. From afar you could not hear the words. It came to us like a deep hum and though the intent of the prayers was as power hungry as any battle, there was something deeply beautiful about it as well.

The praying continued for some time longer and then a wave of white flags were raised through the Christian camp. Along the top of the city battlements, more were flown by the Egyptians. Then there was quiet.

Within his tent the General finally slept.

CHAPTER TWENTY-THREE

We did not understand this scene before us at all. This was an ignorance of war that I was glad to have. Even my short time amongst the army had never shown me anything like this. It was not much longer after that news of the ceasefire reached us.

I looked at Eduardo and smiled.

"It seems Our Lord has paved the way for us to meet with the Sultan."

The next morning we woke and prayed. We ate breakfast and then we began to walk to the city walls. We moved through the Crusader camp, attracting stares and the odd derogatory comment. For the most part though we simply received a nod as a gesture of respect and recognition until we passed by one of the Commanders.

He ran ahead of us and then stood in our path before making us stop.

"Good morning Brothers," he said through a clenched jaw. "Might I ask of where it is you are headed?"

The officers and General had seen us cut through the gathering of soldiers. They knew who we were. Our robes and tonsures were as much of a uniform as their armour and tunics were. Besides, word of my presence always made way around me.

"They have probably come to say prayers with the men," one officer suggested.

The General furrowed his brow. "No. Something doesn't seem right. They are moving like men with an urgent deed to be done. Look how fast and steady they are walking!" He pointed out to them. "They have not stopped once to speak with anyone. Their hands are fast within their sleeves and not laid blessing upon one man."

He watched us intently for some moments more, then he realised the direction we were going led straight to the doorway through which his messengers also walked. When he spoke again his voice was loud and angry.

"They are headed to the gates of the city! Heaven help us! He is seeking audience with the Sultan. He could undo all of this! Stop him! STOP HIM NOW!"

The Commander who had stopped us knew not of this directive from his General. He was just asserting himself and knew his authority was thin at best in doing anything to discipline me.

"Why good morning," I said calmly. "We are making way to enter Damietta."

"I'm afraid I cannot allow this," the Commander tried vainly to declare his power. "You see there is a ceasefire...."

"Yes I am aware of this," I interrupted him on purpose. He was treating us as fools and there was nothing that obliged me to participate with this. "I am also aware that you have no authority over me. I am also aware that as a free man I can walk here as I please and seek entry to whatever city I please to seek audience with whoever I please."

The Commander's face reddened and his eyes glared as I continued on.

"I am also aware that a letter to the Vatican could see you or anyone who tried to impede my work recalled to Rome for discipline."

The Commander stepped aside though his demeanour was clearly now much more hostile than when we had begun. Eduardo and I continued on our way.

"I look forward to seeing your heads sent back to us soon," he spat as we walked past.

We were soon before the door within the gate and pulled upon a cord that rang a bell inside to summon a guard who then peered through a mesh window to look upon us. I saw him scan us up and down, somewhat confused by our robes.

His wariness of just who we were was within his voice as he asked of us, "Who are you and what business do you have in Damietta?"

"I am Brother Francis and this is Brother Eduardo. We are of the Franciscan monks of Assisi and we seek audience with the Sultan," I said clearly and with a steady voice. "We just wish to share the love and joy of God with him."

I expected to have to wait much like we had at our first visit to Rome and this indeed would have allowed the officers opportunity to stop us. Instead the door opened and we stepped through.

"The Sultan has been expecting you," the guard said and bowed his head. We bowed ours in return and as I raised my face I could not help but smile as wide as I was able.

The officers had run down through the troops as fast as they could. They saw us walk past the commander and they saw the door open to let us into the city. They began to yell but they were not close enough to have made any difference. I certainly could not hear them let alone any of the men nearby that could have made good their orders.

The door closed and the officers stopped where they were, breathing heavy. Then one of them walked to the Commander who stood watching the door. The Officer hit him hard upon the shoulder, making the Commander jump and then grab at where he had been struck.

"You fool! Why did you not stop him?" shouted the Officer. "What sort of commander allows anyone to break the front of a ceasefire?"

"He threatened me!" shouted back the Commander.

"A puny man with only a sack upon his body? And you with your armour and sword?"

"He said he could have me recalled to Rome."

The Officer sighed and clenched his fist, raising it as though preparing to punch the Commander, then dropped it down again. He turned and looked at the city.

"He will get his reward soon enough," he muttered and then began to walk back to the General.

"The sooner we endure the General's wrath at not stopping him, then the sooner it will be over," he thought and nodded for the other officers to follow him.

He entered the tent with the other officers close behind him while the General looked among them for me and Eduardo.

"Where is he?" the General asked knowing that he would not like the answer.

"The Commander was threatened by him and told he would be reported to Rome for stopping him. He was within the door before we could reach him," the Officer answered with his head down waiting for his rebuke.

"Oh I know. Do you not think I watched it unfold from here?"

"So you saw that we did our best then?"

The General sighed and closed his eyes. "Yes, despite your best efforts it was quite impossible. So unfortunately I cannot punish you or I would be seen as unjust." The General finished and rubbed at his temple with one hand while the other curled upon the armrest of his chair. "Just make sure their heads are sent to Rome as soon as they are hurled over the wall. I am sure Rome would love to see what became of their favourite sons."

No head made its way over the wall. We were ushered to the Sultan's court and greeted as though we were friends known for a lifetime.

The Sultan even stood with his arms open wide as we walked into the room to meet him.

"Welcome my Christian brothers. What an honour to have such men within my presence," he practically bellowed.

I found this quite amusing and was very curious as to how he knew of us.

"Your brothers have quite a reputation. The ones who work in the Holy Land are doing much to create peace. And here I have the founder within my home. It is as though Allah blesses me with such guests," he continued on.

"It is our honour to be received," I replied and bowed my head as did Eduardo.

We broke bread. We sipped wine. We spoke for hours. The Sultan listened to me speak my faith as I did of his. It was a slow exchange as we waited for the interpreter to convey our conversation. I could sense he was deeply challenged in making sure the truth of our words was relayed. I trusted him implicitly and knew the Lord would help him share just what I had expressed and I believe the Sultan believed this also.

At one stage he looked me up and down. "It is such a relief to see your brown robes after the blue and white of your Crusaders. It makes me feel we can connect with a fresh energy rather than the burden of what has been."

I sighed and smiled when he said this. Then I nodded. "Indeed the past should not determine how we move ahead. Even with what is happening right now and so close by."

The Sultan nodded. "I do hope you realise that I understand this battle has nothing to do with Allah or whatever name we shall give our Holy Father. I call upon Allah to protect us as we guard our way of life. Our blood is within the lands we live upon. I cannot just hand over our home to those who want to destroy our culture and our heritage. That is why I will fight. No God would sit back and sanction such actions by men on their behalf. But I do believe that God will watch over the ones who take up arms to defend their homes and families.

I will not concede to such men who come to lands they have no claim upon. To do so under a proclamation of a teacher who never held a sword is beyond my comprehension. I know this is about power and politics. They make it about God to justify their barbarity and delusions. They will reap their rewards soon enough."

I remained within the city walls for another week as his guest. We were shown to elaborate rooms with beds so soft and high you would want to never leave them on waking. Eduardo came and knocked upon my door soon after we were shown to our rooms.

"Francis, how can we sleep in such a place after our vows?" he asked. "We should go to the barns or servant's quarters."

I shook my head. "As much as I agree, we are in a fragile situation and cannot disrespect his hospitality. Yet within this we can find ways to honour our vows," I offered.

With that I walked to the bed and pulled off the large blanket spread across it. I folded it in two and laid it upon the floor creating a makeshift mattress. Then I took the smallest and flattest of the pillows to complete my bed.

"We ate with him but we did not overindulge. We can sleep within his home in the same way."

Eduardo nodded and went to arrange his own room.

When we left through the gates a week later we did so upon horses with four of the Sultan's guards mounted on horses around us. With thanks to the ceasefire which was still underway, we were all safe to travel. What was even more glorious was that our escort was to ensure us safe passage to the Holy Lands with the sanctioned permission of the Sultan. I would finally make it to the lands upon which Our Saviour had lived and spoken his glorious words. I could do so with absolute surety across land, and not upon a boat.

As was expected our departure was noted and we soon had an envoy from the Crusader's camp come to question us.

"Did you make peace? What has the Sultan conceded to?" I was asked.

"Yes. We made peace between Christian and Muslim. The Sultan concedes to nothing which will compromise his home and traditions," I replied bluntly and imagined what that would conjure amongst the leaders.

While I imagined their reaction I also did not care for their conclusion. I had achieved what I had hoped for in being received by the Sultan. Though part of me would have loved to have seen the entire world embrace Christianity as the pure way to connect with God, I had a new respect for the Muslims. I had been received with joy and respect. I had been shown the utmost hospitality and been offered as much consideration for my beliefs as I had for theirs.

In the end that is the basis of being a Christian, and though they did not venerate Jesus in the way that we did, they still held his values. That let me leave with a heart that was full, even though part of it still ached for the Crusaders to find another way. I had done my part in my integrity and truth. That was all I could do.

Eventually the Crusaders would fail but that would be long after my departure. Onwards to the Holy Lands I went and began one of the most glorious parts of my life.

CHAPTER TWENTY-FOUR

I wept openly when I saw Jerusalem appear before us. It had been described to me so many times that I thought I had a clear image of what it would look like. It was nothing as I had pictured yet was everything I had felt of it. It stood majestically. Despite being battered by man and nature, it had risen over and over to be a beacon to all who held faith in something grander than a simple human existence.

I could barely speak as we finally walked upon the very streets Jesus had as a child and then as an adult. I could feel his presence everywhere calling to me. At times I almost forgot to breathe as I was overwhelmed to see the actual places I had read about or been told about.

We walked into the Church of the Holy Sepulchre and I went to kneel at the anointing stone amongst the other pilgrims. Then we made way to the altar that lay over the site of the crucifixion.

"Do you believe this is the actual site?" Eduardo whispered to me.

I looked at the line of people waiting their turn to stand in what they knew to be the place of Jesus' ultimate suffering. They walked up in silent reverie, in anticipation and clutching onto a faith deep within them that brought them here for a deeper connection to our grand teacher and the Almighty. I saw them weep as they knelt and offered prayers to gain their own absolution and deliverance.

As they walked away I could feel something different within them as though something was changed. For some you could see it in their face. Others it was the way in which they walked. Some of them wept. It was not just about the location. They had all been touched by the humanity of the crucifixion and being here at this holy site had given them a realisation of it that no other place could.

Did it matter whether this was the true place of Calvary? As I looked upon these people who had travelled so far, who had come with their hearts full of his love and now walked away with them overflowing I knew the answer.

"It doesn't matter," I replied.

It truly didn't. If we had indulged our minds with such questions upon the pilgrimage then we would have been distracted from the gifts that being here would offer us. If we stopped and questioned every locale and the story aligned with it, then we would interfere with letting our spirit feel the energy of Jesus that was steeped in every inch of this place.

If we entertained those questions, then it diluted the faith and commitment of those who came. It would feed doubts and fears that would erode the joy of being present to witness and expand our faith. No, I would not feed that uncertainty. Instead I would celebrate the joy of being here.

Though I loved to walk the streets of Jerusalem I loved even more to escape the bustle by climbing the hills around her. It was a pattern I had established well in escaping Assisi as a much younger man and again at La Verna. There is something just delightful about being raised up above normal life. I am sure you could all say there is some symbolism in literally being closer to God and yes that is partly true also.

For me though it is about the quiet that you can allow into your being. You separate from the mundaneness of human life and in that space you can allow a clarity that cannot be with the goings on of day-to-day life which constantly surrounds you within a city or town. The one thing I truly always adored when you were sitting upon that hillside was how you could feel the gentle breezes that were hidden from you down below.

They caressed your skin and soothed you like nothing I had ever felt. I could not compare it to a lover as I had never known one, but it was like the love that a mother would offer a child. I would imagine it was another way of God reminding me of his love. It was also a beautiful way to call me into his arms even deeper.

I found my way to the Mount of Olives alone one day. It was a rare moment that I allowed myself but I knew it was necessary. Once there I stood and felt the breeze wrap around me. It was dry and warm, different to the ones that made their way from the snow capped Apennine Mountains back in Italy. Within that difference I felt something new call to me and it was so deep and strong that I will say it was one of the most defining moments of my life.

The Mount of Olives was the place celebrated as being the site of Jesus' ascension. It was here that he stood surrounded by his apostles forty days after his resurrection and left the Earth to return to the heavens. As the breeze soothed me I knew in that moment that I was standing upon the actual place this had occurred, and for all my posturing about that not mattering, I knew with all my soul that for me in this moment, it most certainly did.

I closed my eyes and felt the presence of Jesus close by my side.

"Show me. Please my Lord. Show me what it was like," I almost begged of him.

I opened my eyes and saw before me a group of women and men standing in a line. They were dressed in ancient robes. The women wore scarves over their heads. The men wore full beards and long hair. All of them smiled at me with such an intense love I could not help but return that smile. Then one by one they placed a hand upon their heart and I saw them all breathe deeply down into their bellies.

Some closed their eyes while others continued to gaze upon me and smile. I wanted to stay here with them forever.

"Why do they look at me like this?" I asked Jesus and that was when I felt the strangest sensation. I no longer felt him beside me. It was as though he had stepped into the very same place that I was standing. I took in a sharp breath as the very thought of such a thing occurring seemed immediately sacrilegious.

"Just take a deep breath as they are," I heard him say and so I did.

That was when something incredible happened. As I took that breath I felt Jesus merge into my body. We no longer shared the space as two beings there. We were now as one. I saw with his eyes. I felt his heartbeat within mine. We shared the same breath.

Now when I looked out to the group before me I could understand why they looked upon me so. They were simply reflecting back the love they could feel from me and it was overwhelming and grand. I took another deep breath and within me I dived into that love. It was infinite and beyond any bounds that my human mind could imagine.

Jesus was showing me the love he had for all humanity and it was so big that I felt my body could not bear to sense it anymore.

"Breathe..." came Jesus' voice from within me and my body seemed to swell to allow even more of that love into my being.

It was rich and delicious. It was comforting and majestic. I wanted to feel it even more but was sure that my simple human condition simply could not accommodate it.

"Breathe..." came his invitation once again and as I did even more of this divine love washed through me.

"I am complete," I called out softly. I was ready to leave this life. There was nothing more I needed to experience as a human in service to God now that I knew this feeling.

It was what I had been searching for my entire life. This sense of bliss that was limitless and unconditional. I had moments of it in prayer but ached to know it more. I had believed that I needed to serve more, to pray more, to teach more when all I had to do was breathe and let it come to me.

"Was this what your whole life was like?" I asked Jesus and I felt a gentle laugh as his reply.

I looked around at the group before me. One by one they started to nod. It was their way of telling me they knew and felt what was within me. They did not need a teacher or guide anymore. They were ready to live as I was in this moment. They were ready to go and teach others.

I smiled upon them one last time and with a deep breath Jesus let me feel what it would be like to release my soul from my body. I felt it swoop and soar above me, spiralling into the heavens. Though my own spirit was still well within my body, it now resided there with a new freedom that was liberating and exultant.

I am not sure how long I was upon the mountain. I was told later it was many hours. I didn't care. I had the most intimate moment with Our Saviour that anybody would ever have. He had shown me with such beautiful simplicity the moment of his ascension and even more profoundly he had let me feel his experience.

Part of me ached to release my body as he had, right in the same place and right now. Yet something else called me to return.

One by one the group before me had turned to walk back down the mountain, slowly disappearing as they did so. I knew in my heart that I must also. They had all returned to humanity to continue Jesus' work. Each one of them carrying with them that intense love that God gifts to each of us. I too had now allowed it within me with even more intensity than ever before.

There was something else that I felt had shifted within me. As I descended the mountain I noticed I was walking differently but that didn't seem so important. I took another deep breath as Jesus had asked of me and called out to him. He answered but I did not hear him as words spoken beside me as I had heard them before. Now I felt him answer as a presence within me. We were no longer separate. We were now blended as one. The Saviour had sent his energy within me and that was the greatest blessing I could ever have been given to continue my work and carry on in this life.

I did not have to seek outside for this love from him. It was eternally a part of me. As God had given Jesus to us, as his son, to be the embodiment of Our Lord upon this Earth, now I was being allowed to carry that Christ energy within myself. This was the culmination of my work, my prayers and my dedication. This was an immense honour to be allowed to know such a connection with God, and it gave me renewed vigour for my service.

I did not speak of it openly at first. It took me some time to fully understand or rather, to feel what had happened. I speak as though I walked back down that mountain with such clarity about what I had experienced with Jesus and the vision of the apostles. In a way my heart sensed it, but my consciousness around the event needed time to settle and adjust to who I had now become.

I understood and knew this intuitively. I thought about Jesus' time in the desert and the immense changes he undertook. He allowed himself time to shift into a new period of his experience and so must I.

I could have shared my experience widely. It could have become part of my mythology and indeed it would have helped people understand the remainder of my life, but somehow it did not feel right to do so. It had been such a deeply intimate moment with Our Saviour that I truly did not want to share it. I could barely put into words what had happened. All I could describe was how it had felt and few would be open to understanding even that.

When I did speak of it with an intimate few, they wept openly and nodded, letting themselves also feel what Jesus had given me. They vowed that they too would make way to the mount, while others confessed they would never be worthy to be allowed such a connection.

That would always be their choice. I am so grateful for what I chose.

CHAPTER TWENTY-FIVE

Elias had been in Jerusalem for some years when I arrived and our order under his leadership flourished and gained more respect as time passed.

"We do not make waves. We just do our work and people come to us," he smiled and I nodded with pride at the values of our order being upheld.

He walked with me to the Holy Sepulchre one morning and we prayed together at the anointing stone. We did so again at the site of the cross and then knelt within Jesus' tomb that is housed further within the church.

I did not pray, nor did I close my eyes. I looked upon the stone bed where Jesus' body had lain; dabbed in oils and wrapped in linens. I felt the care in which his body had been prepared, with the blood of his wounds washed away, so that he lay clean of the cruelty he had endured. I imagined his wounds and how they would be the only symbol of his suffering. Here he would have been in peace and silence.

I pictured the body lying still. No heartbeat, no breath. An eternal rest that all of our bodies would know eventually. Then I imagined the breath of God being sent to that body and pictured the chest once more rising up. Within his chest, his heart would begin to pump again and his eyes would have opened.

Angels would have gathered to support and keep the energy around him clear. They would have whispered to him as he awoke and returned; guiding him as a midwife at a birth would, reminding him of his destiny to serve humanity. Jesus would have smiled as they spoke.

"Of course..." he would have replied. "Of course..."

It was the same words I had felt myself say as I walked back down the Mount of Olives. When I heard the call to return, it was the angels whispering to me to remind me of my service.

"Of course..." I too had replied. "Of course..."

We all have opportunity to be reborn within our life. We all have opportunity to arise from our suffering, no matter how horrific it may seem. Jesus has shown us this through the immense sacrifice he had made in his own death. Within his surrender to the nails and wood of the Romans, Our Saviour had held his faith, his trust and his acceptance. No greater sign of this was his asking of Our Father to forgive the men who enacted his crucifixion.

Then when Jesus cried out with some human despondency asking of God, "Why have you forsaken me?" he was answered not with words. Instead he was answered with a wave of unconditional love that swept him into the acceptance which allowed him to die at peace.

That moment of complete surrender took his spirit in balance and grace. He left not just in peace but with absolute trust for the design that Our Lord had for his story as a teacher. Our Saviour's spirit remained close. He walked amongst the mourners as they watched his body lowered. He watched as his body was washed and anointed. He stepped into the tomb as his own body was placed there and sat by it as the stone was rolled into place to seal the doorway.

Then he waited, and prayed and breathed.

Yes a spirit and soul can breathe as though they have a body. It is not the same physical act though. It becomes a simple conscious connection with all that is. It is the reminder that from whence they came they can return. It is the opening of the eternal wisdoms for guidance and clarity. Thus Jesus sat by his body and breathed.

When the angels arrived to announce it was time to return, Jesus looked upon his body and for a moment thought he might change his agreement, but this was gone in an instant. The joy and freedom of being non-physical would be replaced by the same sensations when he came back to complete his story.

Jesus simply said "Yes" and his spirit once more went into his body.

This is what he shared with me as I knelt within his tomb. Along with my experience upon the mountain I left Jerusalem a very different man. There was no great physical change but people could sense something within me had altered. For most it was simply that I had walked the Holy Lands and been blessed to be in the presence of such important places. Some though saw something much deeper and it inspired many to also make pilgrimage to the most venerated places of our Christian heritage.

I made one last visit to the Holy Sepulchre on my last evening in Jerusalem. The next morning I would make way to the coast to sail back to the Italian shore. I went to the site of Calvary where Jesus had taken his last breath upon the cross.

I knelt and I prayed. I gave thanks and expressed gratitude. Then I looked up and spoke openly, not caring for who might hear:

"My Saviour, what you have blessed me with here has been beyond measure and compare. I have given my life to you with no remorse or regret and you bless me with such gifts that I can now serve you even in grander ways. All I have to give, I give to you unconditionally. All I have to give is my body; that I may speak your words and be your vehicle as you were to your father. Take my body as though it were yours. Use it as you would use your own. I will surrender to however you feel will serve you."

That night I slept soundly but woke abruptly at dawn as though someone had shaken me.

"Do you realise what you promised away to him?" a dark voice deep inside me said.

"Yes," I replied.

"And you are truly willing to surrender with such depths to this promise?"

"Yes," I said again and the dark voice said no more but I felt something hang in the morning air.

I spoke little with Eduardo as we ate at breakfast. We had already made our plans to depart so thankfully there was little we needed to discuss. The Sultan's horses and escorts were still with us, as their work would not be complete until we had boarded our ship. Once more we were upon the horses and now we made away from Jerusalem.

As we reached the very outskirts I looked back and saw the gold dome of the Muslim shrine. I reflected on all that had unfolded since I had travelled to Egypt. It had only been months and yet I felt as though I had lived an entire life within that time.

Eduardo on his horse beside me was feeling the same. "I am not the same man who arrived here," he said quietly.

"Neither am I," I replied. "That, my brother, is a glorious thing."

Eduardo nodded and smiled as we both farewelled the Holy Lands and rode away.

CHAPTER TWENTY-SIX

The interaction and integration with Jesus that I allowed during my Holy Land pilgrimage was to have deep effect on the remainder of my life. In many ways my life would now reflect this from my demeanour through to physical expressions. Thankfully the reflections began in more energetic and emotive ways with the physical ones waiting for some years, or my already seeming short life would have been even briefer.

The greatest gift this blending would bestow on me was the true connection with ultimate compassion. I believed I had already allowed this within my life but after Jerusalem I embodied it in a new way.

Compassion for my time was seen as something akin to pity and sympathy. It was something you offered to a beggar or someone in mourning. Compassion in my religion was the offering of a tithe to support those in service, or the act of saving and protecting the weak and vulnerable. Compassion would open up for me as I now felt it as the energy of acceptance.

It is very easy to hand a beggar some food. It is our nature to cry with someone who has lost a loved one. It is another thing entirely to do these things without some sort of judgement or without wanting to make the situation "right".

To look upon someone who is starving and see this as perfect is something no one can imagine is possible. We have great ideas on suffering and how it is wrong and how it should be eliminated. We try to make sense of death with suggestions of the deceased's age or the reasoning that it was the end of suffering an illness.

Worse still we attribute suffering as punishment from God; that this is divine justice being played out to correct someone's sins or wrong doings. I found this last one particularly disturbing. To suggest a God with all encompassing love for us, who designed us in his image and gave us the glory of life would then punish us in such ways never felt correct. After my pilgrimage this was even more so.

Now I should clarify I still believed in heaven and hell. I certainly believed in an eternal reward for choosing a life of divine connection and acceptance of good, or the alternate for those who willingly chose evil as they lived.

For me now I saw each person living their perfect path with endless opportunities to seek redemption and accept the truth of Our Lord. A time of suffering or loss was an invitation to prayer and the gifts that would bring. It was also that person's choice to stay within their suffering and ill ways.

Though I wished everyone would live full devout lives with God, with no lack and with good health, I too saw the beauty in God's design. For in allowing people to live without faith, to allow them to choose darkness, he created a rich, elaborate tapestry of experiences. I looked upon humanity and saw it was perfect.

Life to me now presented itself as a journey upon which we could choose our destiny in the heavens in eternal glory, or that we should go to infinite darkness. Without the evil and suffering, how could we ever truly appreciate how grand God's love for us was? The journey could be a struggle with temptations and distractions, but for those who chose glorious eternal love it would become a life of warmth, hope and prosperity. It would be that way forevermore.

I looked upon each person and now saw their choices as the gift of freedom that God granted us so that we could design where we would walk and eventually rest. It was now my duty to live within the light and love to inspire others. I could not take everyone into its embrace but whomsoever I did would be a soul that would be celebrated in the heavens.

This acceptance granted upon me a new peace. I was more calm than I had ever been. There was no impulse or urgency to preach; instead I trusted that the souls ready to come back to God would do so when they were ready. All I had to do was stay firm in my commitment and dedication, and to speak the Lord's words from my heart with absolute devotion.

◆ CHAPTER TWENTY-SEVEN

Though I ended my mission works and visits abroad, my brothers continued to travel. More became martyrs but no blood was ever shed by their hands. They arrived in compassion and offered support to the needy. It was only when asked of what compelled them to do so that they spoke. Within their sharing, many they talked to came back to God. It was not always through Jesus though. Some simply returned to the purity of their own religion.

Whoever returns to God is blessed no matter in what religion or practice. Whoever does so with a pure heart and open to receive his limitless love is not only blessed but granted eternal life.

In the unconditional love that is offered by our creator and sowed within our soul is all the strength and courage any man or woman will ever need. This is our fuel to live. It is our redemption and it is our path to joy and wonder.

All things begin with love and all things must return to love. There is no place for struggle or battle within this space. There is just comfort, trust and nurturing.

We receive it as babies and as we grow we forget it is our natural way of being. Yes, it is truly our natural way of being, yet it becomes so easy to lose our way.

God is never happier than when we return to his love. The most wonderful thing is that this love is always within us. All it takes to allow it back into our lives is accepting it.

The grace in which I lived the years following my pilgrimage to the Holy Lands began to be challenged several years later. I had begun to speak openly of my transformation there, as well as simply radiating it so that many wished to visit there now. However the Crusades and other factions had infused even greater unrest since my return. Pilgrims were simply too frightened to want to travel, even with the pride of martyrdom a possibility. Quite frankly I was tired to hear of another death in the name of Our Lord whether as a Christian or otherwise.

Yes, I had an incredible experience but this followed a life of intimate connection with Holy Spirit as well as all my service as a priest. Yes, I knew people had their own epiphanies and enlightenment in their own way when they travelled there. However the risk to do so when they could achieve this, even just similarly, within their own land was too cruel a potential to play with.

Aside from the risks there were many who simply could not afford to do so. Passage and boarding were considerable costs even with hostels or billeting. It pained me even more to see simple people despondent that they could not travel to the iconic sites of Our Saviour.

I prayed upon this for many days. I asked the Lord to show his people that they did not need to see the Holy Lands for their redemption or saving. I prayed he would keep his children safe and let them feel his love wherever they were.

As I was praying one day I suddenly remembered my visit to Bethlehem and when I stood in the place of Jesus' birth. Beneath the basilica to mark the location there was a cave-like sanctuary within which was a simple manger with some animals close by.

I stood there and looked upon this scene and honoured its simplicity and humility. This was how our greatest teacher had begun his life in what you would call poverty and yet it was full of God's love. Jesus never once saw himself as anything less than his truth. He never once used his circumstances to deter or falter from his faith. Yet around me I saw people questioning their own faith due to where they could or would travel.

Within that vision I had my answer. If people could not go to the Holy Lands, then we could create them here. With God's blessing, we would let them see the glory of such places. I imagined recreating Calvary within our own church, a tomb and an anointing stone. Then I felt that all this would be a folly and make light of their truths. There was only one scene that we would need to help people connect and that would be the nativity.

When we take people back to the beginning of a story they can see its essence. It is not clouded by other stories and agendas that get overlaid as it develops and continues. This was why the nativity would become so important in my time.

We headed to nearby Greccio where another chapter of our order was begun by Brother Ferdinando. I wanted a place that had a small grotto, not a cave but just a sheltered space. I could have sought out a barn but that did not feel necessary and besides that would mean using someone's property and that could lead to jealousies as to who I would choose.

No, instead I would seek a natural haven. This in itself would instil one of the greatest attributes as to what I wanted to share and that was the complete lack of any luxuries or indulgences that Jesus was born amidst. Greccio had just the place and within ease of anyone to walk there. It was at the base of a small hill that Ferdinando and others used for retreat at times.

"It is a wonderful quiet place with no distractions," he told me in a message and as I stood there looking back upon the small village I could sense this and more.

I was glad it was not so high up as was my retreat upon La Verna. It helped add the sense of normalcy I also wanted. This would also make it easy to create our scene.

We built a manger and placed it in the centre, filling it with hay. I then pushed it down in the centre so it became like an immense nest. I wiped my hands across each other when I felt that there was enough of a shape for a newborn babe to lie there and couldn't help but smile.

Then we walked the donkey and a goat from the monastery, tethering them either side of this with some well-placed hay for them so that Jesus' crib did not become a meal. Some candles lit within the grotto completed our scene as night began to fall.

"Go and call the people to come and worship here," I said to Ferdinando and the two acolytes who had assisted us.

When they were gone I knelt before the manger and prayed.

"Lord, I hope we have honoured you here," was all I wanted to say.

I stayed in place in some silence and could feel the Christ energy I had integrated in Jerusalem swell up inside me. It felt warm and welcoming as always, but I also felt it expand once again. It spoke with no words, but I could feel the joy at having created the nativity.

I opened my eyes and could see a baby within the manger. Beside it sat Mary, while Joseph stood behind her with one hand on her shoulder. Behind me I could feel the Magi and shepherds who came to adore him. I turned to look at them and instead saw dozens of villagers holding lanterns to light their way. They had come to worship Our Saviour in a whole new way. I smiled and my eyes filled with tears.

They began to sing a hymn and my tears now flowed freely as I stood and joined their song. I could see someone pushing through them and it was Ferdinando, holding some wine and the holy sacrament.

"They all came! We must say mass!" he said with more excitement than I have ever seen in any of our brothers.

Ferdinando led the mass and it was wonderful and filled with so much joy. When he gestured to me to say the sermon I did not hesitate.

"My brothers and sisters, how grand it is for you to be here. How grand it is that you honour your faith. How grand it is that you allow the love of God, His Son and the Holy Spirit into your lives," I began.

I turned and gestured to the manger.

"We are all born of the same. We are all gifted life from our creator with love and compassion. No matter the circumstance of our beginning we are God's children. It is the trials of this world that make us believe otherwise. The farmer is no less loved than the nobleman. The king is no grander than the beggar in the eyes of the Lord. So it was that he sent his son to remind us."

I paused and caught my breath as I felt Jesus' energy well up within me.

"Tell them, tell them," he urged me and I turned to the gathering as tears filled my eyes once more.

"Our heavenly Father sent his son here without favour of riches, without the advantages of a noble family. Yet he sent him rich with a heart full of love and honour for all mankind. He came with a commitment to remind us that we have all the wealth we need within us. That the comfort and guidance we need is within us. We need not look outside, or search for God's love and its rewards. All we need is to accept it is within us and is just waiting for us to allow it within our lives."

I could sense that this was beyond some people to comprehend. I could feel their questions start within their minds. I took a deep breath.

"Jesus guide me now," I asked of him and then I let the words begin again.

"Let us pray," I suggested. "For within the peace and grace of prayer we allow that love to come forth. Pray to connect with God and ask for the sense of his love to become greater. Pray that you will not be distracted by the designs of life that cause struggle and make you question the very love that you are worthy of. Let us pray now. Let us do this in silence. Find your own words. Find your own connection that you may walk away from our gathering and know you can do this in every moment."

I stopped talking and people closed their eyes and bowed their heads. Some knelt upon the ground and I decided to also. We all prayed in our own way and as we did so I could sense Jesus walking amongst them. He would stop and touch each and every one of them as he passed by. Not as though he was blessing them, but just so they had an opportunity to feel his presence.

It reminded me of the vision I had when I saw him amongst the wounded in Perugia during the war. This was something so different though. Jesus was not here to heal any wounds. This time he was here in pure joy.

I left the congregation in peace a few more minutes before I continued.

"My friends, my brothers and sisters, as you look upon the manger today remember the humble beginnings of our Saviour." I walked to stand behind it and faced out to them, raising my open hands. "Our heavenly Father sent his son as a king but not as we know a king to be. He sent him as a teacher and he taught us in a way no other teacher has. Most importantly, he sent him as a man as ordinary as you and I. He sent him thus to show us that we can live in the light and love of Our Father no matter our wealth and circumstance. We are all God's children and his love is ready and waiting for us.

Praise be to Jesus for the life he lived to teach us love and compassion. Praise be to Jesus for the sacrifice of his death to lead us to never give up our trust and faith in God. Praise be to Jesus for his resurrection to show us the power of God and that we can always be reborn of our sins within his love and glory. Praise be to Jesus for his ascension so that we too can aspire to live eternally within the splendour of Our Father's love."

"Praise be to Jesus," people began to call back, some as a whisper and some much louder.

I smiled and put my right hand to my chest.

"Praise be to all of you that choose Jesus to be in your life."

With that I turned to Ferdinando and nodded my head, signalling for him to finish the mass. He hesitated and shrugged his shoulders as though he did not know what he should even be doing. He came to my side and leant in close.

"Brother, how can I go on after this?" he pulled back and smiled.

I returned his smile, looked back to the gathering and once more raised my open hands in peace.

"Go now to your homes. Go now with full hearts and the remembrance that you are all God's children."

With that they all began to make their way home.

Ferdinando waited until the last ones had turned to walk away before coming to my side once more.

"That was remarkable. Of all the sermons I have ever seen you give that one was beyond anything you have shared. It was as though a new voice spoke through you," he said.

I nodded. Indeed a new voice had spoken through me. I had invited it when I called upon Jesus. It was his voice I had allowed. Yes it was still me talking, but I had allowed the Christ energy within my voice. I now felt my connection to this energy grow even stronger.

"I allowed Jesus to speak through me," I said simply. "I allowed his love and joy to be within me and to express its truth."

Ferdinando looked at me with eyes wide open now. I could feel him wanting to ask how I had done this and wondering if he could also. Then

171

he suddenly dropped his head and wringed his hands.

"I will never be as worthy as you to know such a thing," he mumbled. "None of us will. You have served more deeply and been more blessed than any of our brothers."

I grabbed at his shoulders. "Look at me!" I demanded and he looked up fearfully. "That is what the darkness wants you to believe; that I am more special, that you need to travel to sacred lands."

Ferdinando shook his head. "No my brother, you were chosen by God for this."

This made me laugh out loud and Ferdinando now looked as though he was angry with me for making light of his insight.

"God did not choose me. I chose God. That is my blessing. That I chose just as you did. The difference is how we choose. I chose with the absolute willingness to shed everything that would distract me from being closer to him. I invite his love and wisdom everyday with every fibre of my being. I know you do too..."

"So why do I not seem to feel or speak it as you do!" Ferdinando interrupted me.

"Because there is something within you telling you that you are not worthy." The words were out of my mouth before I had even realised I had said them.

Ferdinando began to cry and I put my hands upon his shoulders once more, but with gentleness.

"Brother, it is a universal struggle. Every man and woman who stood here tonight has the same voices within them telling them they are no equal to Jesus. That is our role to remind them that they are. And in reminding them, we remind ourselves. We just have to choose how willing we are to remember as grandly as God would wish we do."

Ferdinando gathered himself and began to nod.

"Come let us go eat and then take rest. You and I both know that tomorrow we will have twice the amount of people here to pray with us."

I was wrong about that. Three times the amount of people arrived and we had to hold mass several times a day to accommodate them as even more began to arrive from nearby villages, towns and cities to see the nativity and hear my sermon. This continued on until Christmas Day a few weeks later.

As our gatherings grew I sent word for others to create their own presepios with what resources they had and congregations gathered there also for their priest's unique take on the humble beginnings of Our Saviour.

From such a simple idea this grew and grew. Nativities are now all over the world and in much more elaborate ways than my hay-filled manger flanked by a donkey and goat. I so hope that when someone gazes upon them that something within them is reminded that our greatest teacher began as simply as we all did, and that grandeur and wealth have nothing to do with money but everything to do with what we hold in our hearts.

CHAPTER TWENTY-EIGHT

As time passes and we allow our experience to expand it can outgrow even that which we feel we can comprehend.

It was one year after the nativity in Greccio when I came to realise with a sudden new awareness as to the actual size of our order and how it had grown with a new rapidity in more recent years. The size of the order was not such an issue. How could the increase in number of teachers and the people they could influence ever be a problem.

Unfortunately we were now having issues with the simple concept of management. As the order grew and we spread apart geographically our agreements and vows as to how we lived became even more important to maintain the integrity of the order and how it would serve. This would seem simple but men love to make things complicated.

When we began the Franciscans I was seen as the leader of sorts and this was necessary. I was recreating how we connected with God within the Church structure. It was a new way of even running a monastery. All brothers turned to me for how we would do things. As time went on and the order grew I knew I had to hand over responsibilities to others as I simply could not do all that was required. Besides if I solely lived as an administrator then I would not have the joy of serving mass, counselling, mission work or even to take retreat in prayer.

I shared out duties as was appropriate: one brother to oversee our gardens, one to administer tithes and then their distribution, another to deal with correspondence and so on. Unfortunately what became a necessity to allow our community to function soon became its challenge. You see our brothers joined us with a passion to serve and this virtue served us all so well that when I handed them a duty they carried it out with an almost extreme devotion. That sometimes came at the expense of another's duties.

"Francis, we need to buy some seeds. Our last crop simply suffered too much in the heat."

"Francis I cannot allow such spending when we need to save for buying feed for the animals in winter."

You can imagine the conversations and meetings that were had when I wasn't there to keep them in balance. Though in truth such things I knew were small and human, and with divine invitation could soon be sorted. Our brothers were not averse to being called back to their faith as means to dissolve what was always ultimately a minor dispute.

What really became a concern was that in the beginning of our order all brothers began in Assisi. They had first come from the town and then they came from all over Italy. Then they came from other lands. Saint Anthony of Padua came to join us from Portugal, following the bodies of our first martyrs as they were carried home from Morocco. They all knew to come to Assisi and begin here.

Now as our order spread across Europe and into the Middle East and North Africa, it was not seen as so necessary. Indeed why spend the time and money when they could begin their service almost immediately and in their homeland with knowledge of the local language and culture. It would not serve anyone to make it such a prerequisite. That would be the same as if we all had to travel to Rome.

Ah Rome! When I thought of Rome then my heart would squeeze and tighten. I thought of all the factions within our church and how they all served their own purposes now. I thought of the Crusades and the blood being spilled in Jesus' name. I thought of all the wealth and luxuries the church had gathered so that aspiring to a higher office through service was seen as being rewarded with comforts a simple village priest might not ever know.

I shuddered when I imagined that happening not only in Jesus' name but also in mine and of the order. We began to have meetings to discuss these kinds of topics and they did not always go so well. They were rife with fears and overprotection; all the very things I hated in the structure of the church.

Yes I wanted to be able to hand the order over to God to protect and I did. However that does not always balance out the actions of men driven by their own desires and interpretations of our vows. It also doesn't erase the differences in opinions that men can have over the same matter.

"We simply must have all new brothers begin here in Assisi!"

"No, no, no, we elders can travel to ordain them!"

"Surely we just become far more stringent with those we send to begin and run these orders so they are clear to induct new brothers without question?"

"And this is not how things are now? Do we insult these men already in the outposts by saying we do not trust their judgement and supervision?"

As I sat and listened I saw each point as valid and with merit. Within my own mind and heart I could now see what was needed.

The written word can be open to interpretation. Our very own bible had suffered as such, but this was not due to how it was originally written but more so in how it had been translated and altered over time due to different languages. Aside from this it was never written by those who had taught its words but by those who followed after. I was now in a position to write a guide for our order in a language we all used, written by its founder and overseen by its elders. There would be no question as to what was set out within its text.

This was how we created our "First Rule", though at the time it was merely known as "The Rule Without a Papal Bull", as it was our own edict of how Franciscan life should be and it was not officially approved by the Pope. We did not seek approval. It was not necessary as the guide simply stated all that we had already agreed to live by, and this in essence was already well approved of.

All I simply did was put in writing our pledge to poverty and service to God. I defined how this life would look and how to maintain it. As well we outlined how a monastery should be run and maintained. When one read this there was no question as to how someone choosing to be a part of our order should now spend their life.

Several years later I revised this into the "Second Rule". This time with all the basic formalities covered I could focus more on our dedication to serving God and his gospel. After three years of seeing the first rule being shared across the regions and knowing that a sense of balance and clarity was being lived in all our different monasteries, it felt right to let it expand.

The "First Rule" had made clear our basic way of life and addressed issues of managing ourselves. Three years had been long enough to allow those energies to establish and be grounded. The "Second Rule" expressed in much more depth our commitment to God. Even more perfectly it was now ready to be sent to Rome where it immediately was given approval by Pope Honorius III.

The Franciscan order that had arisen from such humble beginnings was now beyond flourishing. It stood with its own strength and vision. A sense of completion washed through me when the papal decree arrived in Assisi. My eyes filled with tears and I went immediately to our main chapel in the Porziuncola and placed the letter with its crumbled seal upon the altar.

I placed both hands upon it and looked up at the figure of Jesus nailed to his cross that hung upon the wall behind the altar. He looked down on me and though his face had been carved to depict sorrow there was also a peace and acceptance within it as well. I recalled when I sat within the cathedral at Assisi and looked upon the image of Jesus being crucified as he looked up to the heavens. Then I had felt he should have

177

been looking down upon us, to connect with us in our sin and remind us his suffering was and always will be for us. Here I stood now, within the church my faith and service had built, and it was so.

I turned and looked about the chapel with its beautiful windows, its high ceiling and the rows upon rows of carved pews. Part of me should have been overwhelmed as I reflected on how the small crumbling chapel at San Damiano in which I had first served within had supported and allowed this grand place to be built.

I should have knelt at the altar and prayed but instead I sat upon the highest of the steps that lead to it and looked down the body of the church. Leaning forward I put one hand within the other and rested my forearms upon my knees. I bowed my head and replayed all that had happened since I had given my life to God.

I saw all the men and women who had laid their faith not just in God but in me and how they all now served with such grace and glory. They too had transformed as much as this chapel and within their shift they now showed others that they could do so too. Breathing deeply I felt into how I had changed.

This made me smile. For at first I felt nothing had changed. I was the same as I was when I first heard God ask me to rebuild his church. My faith had never faltered, only grown stronger since then. I pushed back further into my life to before this time and saw that the core of who I was had always been there. It had just taken some time to become clear and find its purpose and truth.

God had always been with me. Jesus had always been within me. My faith and commitment had allowed them a voice and expression.

So in that moment as I sat upon the stairs of the altar I gave deep thanks. Yes I gave thanks to God for his guidance in supporting our order. I gave thanks to Jesus for leading the way of being a grand teacher. Then I thanked myself for being strong enough to allow the truth of me to be the way of my life.

I had not pushed it under what my family expected of me. I had not succumbed to a shallow life, lured by riches, wealth or sex. Instead that voice within me that called me to God since I was a child had been heard. That voice is within us all. It is our choice to hear it. I thanked every fibre of my being that I had chosen to hear it.

For in my choosing to hear I had allowed such a magnificent life. As I stepped into my truth it showed others that they could choose this also. They did, by the thousands. They served in my order or with Clare's and they shone a magnificent light that in turn led their congregations to want their own inner light and truth to be set free.

No, this did not overwhelm me. It made my heart swell and my soul sing.

All was well in the world, simply because I had let myself listen to God.

Chapter Twenty-nine

With the "Second Rule" in place I now truly felt I could step back from the more public affairs of the order. It was a wonderful opportunity to know more private time and the delightful silence this could offer me. If you like, I felt this time now was my reward for all the human work I had done to establish the brotherhood and sisterhood. It was also now the time to truly dive in even deeper to my connection with God.

It may seem the blessings bestowed upon me and the order would have proven that my connection was more than complete. Many see their relationship with God as finite, as something to simply accept into their life. For me I saw it as an ever expanding invitation. The more I allowed God into my life, then the more room I had for his love and guidance. For me each day was an opportunity to become even more of his servant.

So I prayed more. I stayed in silence more. My meetings with the priests became scarcer and I rarely offered mass or spoke the sermon. I retreated more and more into my personal space and the delicious reverie of communing with the Holy Trinity.

I heard God's words clearer than ever. I felt Jesus within me become bolder. The Holy Spirit washed me with a warmth that grew stronger. It was said that just to walk past me was as though that person felt God's presence beyond anything experienced in prayer. This was quite true. I had chosen to be the embodiment of God's love, Jesus' teaching and the compassion of the Holy Spirit. I had chosen it with such a fervour and passion that my life simply had to be the manifest of this choice.

There was nothing strong enough to distract me or tempt me from their embrace. This was the seemingly simple choice of my existence and thus became my experience. The joy and grace it offered me was beyond anything I could explain. Instead I would simply walk and radiate my presence so that would inspire others in their choice to allow God into their life.

We were forty days from Michaelmas, the grand celebration of the quartet of Archangels. We exalted Michael for his strength, Raphael for his infinite trust, Gabriel for bearing the truths of our Lord and Uriel for gifting us the embrace of divine love. We called upon them to protect and guide us within our small human world. They were created as God's highest servants, to lead us and remind us that though we were small, we could be as divine as they with the right choices.

I walked to my beloved Mount Verna for retreat. I wanted forty days of true solitude and separation so that in turn I could commune with the infinite energies of the divine and embrace my connection even more. Orlando walked with me to the clearing outside the cave.

"I know you seek to fast but perhaps I could leave a basket here every few days. I am sure the Lord does not wish you to suffer so," he almost pleaded with me.

"A simple skin of water will suffice. My body will need of nothing else but God's love until I return," was my reply.

There is no suffering in turning away from comforts and human needs when you do so with a heart that is pure and a mind that is clear. To give up food, bathing and my bed were not sacrifices. Sacrifice implies a debt being settled at a greater cost to the one offering than that which is asked of them. I saw no cost in giving up my human needs to take retreat, for I knew I would be gifted in more wonderful ways.

The first few days of retreat for me were always the same. My mind and body needed to settle. My stomach would rumble. My ears would want to listen to the bird song outside. My skin would cool and then I would shiver. My mind would try to distract me with wondering how the monastery was without me. I would smile and remember all was well.

These were such small things. So small. I was choosing much grander for my experience. I did enjoy their presence in those first days though. They reminded me of how human I was, and how we all are. It reminded me of the distractions that each day play upon people within their lives and how it kept them from the pure love within them.

Each distraction came to me like a blessing with its story and its gravity. Each distraction was opportunity to call out to God even stronger and make my resolve more deep. Each moment that called to me, that wanted me to question what I was doing, was also an invitation to show how dedicated I was.

Four days and all was settled. The energies of my mind and body were now reset and aligned with my choice for the retreat. I fell into a bliss that I might not ever leave. It was in this state that I knew I was wide open to receive all I could. In that moment of realising that I was now within this grace something inside rose up like a lion's roar.

"Holy Father, your Son and the Holy Spirit, I am now free to hear you without the shackles of the mind. I am open to your love and guidance. I give myself to you completely. Show me. Teach me. Use me in any way you can. My heart and body are yours."

I was not sure if I said the words out loud. That was not important anyway. What was important was that I declared them from my very soul. There was no hesitation nor was there any expectation as to what that would invite. That was when I truly felt all the energies within me and around me grow so huge it was like a wave of water began to fall down heavy upon me.

It was so intense that I had to catch my breath. I straightened my back and breathed the deepest breath I could and the energy dissipated and became the opposite. I felt the walls of the cave become like paper that was translucent. The hardness of the stone beneath me became soft and then it was as though I floated above it. The darkness became filled with colours that swirled and ebbed and flowed.

"I am no longer of this world..."

It was a thought but not of my mind. It was a sensation that rippled through me. Then the grandest of all feelings made its way.

I became free of time.

This was a new sensation for me and I was now in a deep state of consciousness that was well beyond the simple state of meditation, prayer or reflection. I surrendered to it and it carried me like a babe in its waves and caresses.

There no longer was any definition of any kind. Not physical, mental or emotional. I was not just being offered a greater connection to God. I was now all-knowing of his energy. There no longer was Francis calling out to God. No longer was he observing me or I of him. We were one and the same.

I understood finally.

I was his embodiment. Just as Jesus had been. I was his vessel to act out his love, to share his compassion and to know his joy. As we all were.

God was simply waiting for us to allow this knowing into our lives.

I smiled and tears fell down my cheeks, for despite my expanded consciousness I was still connected to a body. Then I rejoiced in the moment for it meant I was still also connected to my life as Francis and my life as a teacher. I could now walk the Earth with the knowing that I had just allowed. That to me was the greatest gift I could imagine giving not only to myself but to those around me.

Blessed are those who know God. Even more blessed are those who allow his love and joy into their lives.

Blessed are those who serve God. Even more blessed are those who choose to serve by embodying his grace in their actions.

Blessed are those who seek a pure life. Even more blessed are those who do so hand in hand with the soul God granted them.

Our souls, for so long seen as that energy gifted us by God. I knew now that soul was God alive within us. When we embrace soul, we embrace God and his love.

It is that energy within us that is infinite and beyond definition, yet can shape our existence. In that small, dark and cold cave I found the truth of God. Even grander, I found the truth of my soul and it was glorious.

Each day of my retreat now was simply diving deeper into this knowing and this truth. The huge influx of energy that had opened up my consciousness settled into a more human frequency and I was once more fully connected to the physical world around me as well as my body. I did not see this as any sort of compromise for what I knew and truly felt now. I saw it as a necessity to function and exist in a way that would fulfil my choice to be a teacher of God's truth.

I had heard many stories of the ancient holy men and seekers who took retreats in isolation. Many never returned, choosing to perish rather than go back to ordinary life. Some returned but never were able to adjust or assimilate their new wisdom with the everyday requirements to simply be a functioning adult. Invariably they would then live separately from society, with some creating communes or mystery schools.

I recall when hearing such stories that this gaining of wisdom and enlightenment seemed almost futile and a waste. What was the purpose of gaining such experience if you could never share it or even live a fulfilled life with it? Perhaps hiding in a commune was rewarding enough for them but I could not imagine it would ever be for me.

Those who left this life, or rather simply allowed their death, were also a puzzle to me. We had heard all the stories of those who "ascended" upon their enlightenment, and indeed Jesus had shown me the moment of his. For me the word ascension since that time on the mount had come to mean completion. Jesus had shown me how complete he had been with his experience. So indeed, many of these other seekers may simply have felt complete and hence their transition.

I knew I was far from complete. Even when I reflected upon what I had achieved and the legacy that I had well and truly established, I simply wanted more of my life. My life was so filled with joy and love. Now I had allowed even more of the grandeur this gifted me and I wanted to know it even more. That meant I would need to keep breathing.

So I did. I kept breathing and drank up the beauty of my life.

CHAPTER THIRTY

As days flowed into each other I began to talk with God. To use the word "talk" is somewhat misleading. I was shown visions, given new body sensations and only sometimes were words even used. Many expected me to come back from my retreat with some grand message as had Moses: these people were always very disappointed in me. Those who knew I had simply sought the solace of God's embrace were not, for they saw and felt it within me.

It is said my stigmata began their presence upon the festival of the Exaltation of The Cross and this would make a wonderful synchronicity. As I had lost all track of time I can neither confirm nor deny this. All I can tell you is what happened as my memory can recall it.

As you know I began this retreat by giving myself completely to God as he would see fit to use me. It was not the first time and it would not be the last. To me each time I made this commitment to Our Lord I invited more of the connection to him. So far I had the glorious experience of the dimensions falling away and knowing his presence in a way so few will ever allow.

Now as I swam in the afterglow of this I gave myself over again to his will.

"Grant me the strength to walk this Earth without any denial of all I have allowed with you. Guide me to be the embodiment of all you have shown me. Let me be your gift to the ones who need awakening."

In truth the words came to me in a way in which I had not formed any words before. It was as though they came from within without my mind even taking the time to shape them. To me this made them so pure that I knew it would invite a miracle to take with me to the world outside.

It was late afternoon and that time when the sun seems to hasten its fall to the horizon. This was also the time that occasionally my body would seem to invite me to lie down and rest completely, but I never would for I knew that was idle distraction. Instead I would breathe deeper, stretch a little, perhaps even walk the few paces the cave would allow. Then I would sit back down and begin with some prayers.

On this day I fell into a silence so deep that it felt like the darkness around me grew even blacker and thicker. Then even though my eyes were closed I could feel some light begin to appear. I opened my eyes and it was as though something had torn into the darkness before me.

Through the rip in the black the brightest of light burst through with such intensity I shielded my eyes from it.

I knew it was not light from the cave opening. This was grander than even the sun and despite its intensity, it was not scalding, but shared a soothing warmth with me. Then the brightness settled and within its residual glow I began to sense a shape within it. It became clearer and clearer until I was looking upon the scene of a man being crucified.

There was no mistaking the cross and it appeared in its full size. Upon it was a man, his arms outstretched with his wrists nailed in place, as were his feet one before the other on the central post. He was clothed in elaborate robes of red and gold that were crisp and new, making me wonder why he was not in the simple loincloth as Jesus had been upon his cross.

As I looked up to his face I realised why. There stretched from behind his shoulders and arching up on either side of his head were two massive wings of pure white feathers. They moved slightly and I saw them flex and then relax. Around his head gold light framed his face in a perfect halo. Two more wings sat still across his shoulders while yet another two draped down framing his legs.

If the cross could have only disappeared I would have looked upon the pure form of a seraph; God's greatest servants. I put myself upon my knees immediately and bent forward in servitude waiting for him to address me but he remained silent.

I looked back up into his face and saw how much pain he was in, and yet at the same time he seemed to be in adoration of me much as I was of him. I searched into his eyes for some meaning as to why he would appear to me thus but still I heard nothing. Instead I saw his face offer me even more love.

"Why would you come to me in such suffering?" I asked and still there was no response.

I wanted to reach up and pull at the nails to free him but I knew that would not be possible. Instead I simply looked upon him with awe and reflected upon his circumstance. This I knew would let me connect to his lesson or message. Once I surrendered to this then I felt compassion within me rise up and be offered to him.

"I know you do not truly suffer for you are an angel, and no angel truly suffers," I conceded.

I looked into his face and once more saw the adoration he offered me.

"You see my human suffering as the same," I said and it was not a question.

This made the seraph smile and his wings fluttered ever so slightly.

We create suffering from so many reasons and each of us have great stories around our own experiences with it. It creates a great hierarchy of who deserves the most pity and reward. In essence it is just our choice with how we choose to be. It is but just one part of the illusion that we are godless and are destined to bear hardships.

It is unfortunate that our grandest teacher taught through one of the greatest acts of agony, so that to endure adversity had become for many the way to become one with God. If only people realised Jesus was one with God before his crucifixion and this act had simply shown us how willing he was to never deny this.

There is so much fear in accepting our connection to God, especially when Jesus was killed for speaking this truth. Yet the beauty of what this allows will always outweigh any outcome - even death. There is nothing final in choosing the love we can have from God. Nothing at all. It is but the key to allowing all we can be.

As all this opened up within me I saw the cross dissolve and the seraph now hovered above me, his six wings pulsing in a peaceful rhythm. Then they stopped and he glided gently to the ground before me. With his hands by his side he walked to me and knelt before me as his wings folded behind him.

I dropped my head out of some instinctive fear, but he took my chin in one hand and lifted my face. Now I looked so closely upon him that I could see every lash upon his eyes. We both smiled and then he took my left hand in his right and placed it upon a wound on his left wrist. It was where the nail had held his arm in place upon the cross.

It was hot and almost burned my hand. He then swapped my hand into his left and I felt the matching wound on his right arm. Tears began to fall from my eyes and my body shook but the seraph didn't falter as he now took my right hand and placed it upon his side just below his ribs. The robes there were wet with blood and I knew beneath them was a gash just as Jesus had received from the spear of a soldier to help end his pain upon the cross.

I now fell forward sobbing. I did not cry for the seraph. I did not cry for Jesus. I cried for all those that continued to suffer as they searched for meaning in life. I cried for those who would live a life with no beauty or love in it.

The seraph gently touched the top of my head and then I felt his hand move away. When I looked up he was gone. I curled up on my side and slept until morning.

When I woke the next day I knew my retreat was complete. I walked slowly to the cave entrance and stood there for a few minutes letting my eyes adjust. I laughed out loud as I remembered when I walked free from my prison cell and the sun had seemed so harsh that day. This day it was gentle and as though it was beckoning me to return to life.

When I stepped outside I stretched as I took in the fresh brisk air of the new day. I had been outside before this to relieve myself and trade my canteen of water but those times had been different. My energies were still locked into that of the retreat so I had barely connected with the world outside. I wouldn't have even noticed if someone had been standing there such had been my focus.

Today I looked about me and I smiled upon the trees, seeing their beauty with a refreshed set of senses. The breeze played upon my skin and it was then I felt the sensations within my body.

It was my wrists that first made themselves known as they felt as though something burned into them. I remember lifting them before me and looking incredulously upon the marks. At first I thought it was some dirt that had stuck upon me and I wiped at each one but they would not shift and instead the burning sensation turned into a deep ache. As I looked at them now I saw they were almost identical in nature and position upon each arm.

It was then that I felt the same burning at my feet. Looking down I saw similar marks and I now bent over to touch them. They were the same, though the mark upon my right foot was slightly larger. These started to ache with the same intensity as the ones upon my wrists. I straightened up and took a deep breath which elicited a sharp pain in my right side. I hardly had to reach down as I knew I would feel my own blood weeping from a wound there.

I realised that the seraph had been sent from God so that I too could carry the wounds of Our Saviour. While a very human part of me was yet to understand this, my soul sang with elation.

I did not make such grand news of this, not even to Orlando as I bid him farewell and climbed upon the cart which would carry me back to Assisi. By the time I did arrive back at the monastery I was in incredible pain and all I wanted for was my bed.

My brothers came rushing to greet me and I feigned a smile.

"How was your time Francis?" Bernardo asked as he helped me from the carriage.

"It was truly wondrous," I replied but my grip upon him would not release for I actually feared I might collapse from the pain in my body.

Bernardo saw this in my eyes but assumed I was simply weak from fasting.

"We must get you to the dining hall," he said.

I shook my head. "No I need to rest. A few more hours without food will not be such an issue after so many days."

So Bernardo and another walked me to my chamber and I finally could rest my aching body. The men left me with promise to check upon me soon and then I closed my eyes to pray. The pains did not leave me and that was when I too decided that I needed food. As though he had heard Leo appeared before me carrying a tray with a bowl of soup and some bread.

"You simply must eat Francis," he said. "Have some soup. It will be gentle upon your stomach after all this time."

I slowly lifted myself to sit up and as I did so the sleeve of my robe slid along my right arm revealing the marks upon my wrist. Leo saw it and furrowed his brow.

"How did you sustain such a wound in the cave? Did you fall?"

I looked down at my arm and the mark seemed even larger now. I began to weep and told Leo everything. I showed him my other wrist and was about to show him my feet when he gasped out loud. There was no need to show him the wound on my side as there was enough blood upon the sheets to suggest it. Leo ran for Brother Aldus who was our physician.

Aldus lifted my robe to reveal my side and shook his head.

"There is no break in the skin, yet it is wet," he spoke as though thinking aloud. "This makes no sense Francis."

I knew that. I also knew he could not stop the bleeding. No one could. I was taken from Sienna to Cortona to Nocera and no physician could explain the bleeding or relieve me. The pain and the blood loss that accompanied my stigmata were now part of my life.

In truth I accepted this within the first week. I would recall how this had been bestowed upon me and I would surrender to the seemingly double-edged blessing that I had been granted. Then the pain would crash down upon me like a tidal wave. I would be bedridden and feel useless. That was when I would allow the others to persuade me to seek aid.

In Siena another layer arrived in that my eyesight began to deteriorate. As the world faded around me I realised my time in this life was about to close. Perhaps in asking so much of my retreat I had allowed more than a humble man could endure.

Yet within this I did not see myself as suffering. There is the old ad-

191

age that God will only bestow upon you that which you can bear. Though I was in pain I did not falter in my love for God or Christ. I did not question my circumstance as anything but playing out God's plan and reward for my service.

It was in Nocera I realised that I had succumbed though to the expectations of those around me. They were expecting me to heal and be active again. They were expecting a miracle to manifest within my body. They did not realise I was already living the miracle of God's blessing.

Each day I looked upon the stigmata I was reminded of Jesus' sacrifice for us. Each day I felt the pain in my body I remembered the angel on the cross and how through his own pain he offered me his adoration and compassion. Each day I offered myself these blessings anew.

This did not heal me as one would expect in the usual way of one's body restoring itself but it radiated an acceptance that others began to honour, so that when I said "No more healers" they nodded in agreement.

"What do you wish for now my brother?" Leo asked.

"Take me to my sister Clare. I want to see my beloved San Damiano and my sister," I replied.

Clare sat with me in the chapel when I arrived.

"Do you remember when you found me here after the mass?" she asked with a laugh.

"How could I ever forget!" I laughed in return.

"I think of that day and it seems like that was another person who came to find her way here," she said quietly.

I recalled my first time in this place. The building was derelict and abandoned. Yet God's voice was clear and strong when he told me to rebuild his church.

"We have done all we were asked of. We have done all we were chosen to do," I said just above a whisper but Clare heard and turned her head to look at me.

"You have done even more Francis. You have done more than was asked of you," she said with an intensity that made me recall her younger years. "You are complete in your service Francis. It will be fine for you to seek respite from this life."

Her breath caught slightly as she spoke these last words but they were so filled with love I felt the honour within them and nodded.

"Yes. I am complete," I replied.

Clare nodded. "Good. Then take rest here. You can have the hut to yourself."

The hut stood beside the chapel. It was made from reeds and was simple and beautiful. The bed was plain yet enough. Though Leo and Bernardo refused to leave my side I felt exquisitely alone and at peace to be there.

I would sleep long hours and eat meekly. My body still in pain managed to find a balance that had evaded it since I had left La Verna. My side still released blood but it slowed. Then one day in this new peaceful scenario some words came to me like a song and "The Canticle of The Sun" was born.

I recited it to Leo who then sang the poem back to me. Each time he did I added a new verse. We would laugh as we did so and the delight of playing with creativity this way gave me a fresh sense of joy.

I could have stayed there until my death and it would have been fitting to end my days where they had truly begun, but something deep inside pulled at me to return to the monastery. As complete as I felt I was with life I wanted to end my time there.

San Damiano had refreshed me though and despite being far from what you would call healthy, I had enough vigour to travel the short distance without remorse or need for recovery once I arrived. In some ways I felt as though I was restored, yet the expressions of the brothers when I arrived told me that my appearance did not reflect what I was feeling inside.

I was still aware of what those around me expected though and this did not affect me. However my body was slowly growing weaker despite my acceptance and peace with my condition. Soon I was confined to my bed.

CHAPTER THIRTY-ONE

I thank God and myself that my final months were those of summer and autumn. This meant I could leave my window open to hear the hymns of mass being sung and the birdsong, both of which I adored and gave me great comfort as I lay upon my bed. My eyesight had now reduced everything to a grey haze within which shapes moved around me. The limits of my body now invited me to enjoy the stillness in whatever way I could and my ears became everything.

I heard the distant sounds of farm animals. I smiled when I heard the bells of the tower calling people to mass. I sighed when I heard whispers of brothers outside my door, fearing they would disturb me. Even though my body seemed to be making my world smaller, when I dived into the senses that still were functioning it was just as large as it had ever been.

This was even more so when I closed my eyes and recalled that time within the cave when all the limits of this world had fallen away. I tried so hard many times to go back to that moment but I could not. I understood why this was so. No man or woman can be in such a state and still be contained within a body. I had to choose to stay in that energy or be alive within my body and I had chosen the latter.

From my state now in complete ascension I understand this even more. The world as it was would not have supported me in that condition. Even as I was, I felt my consciousness struggle to be within the world. Every time I recognised how differently I was now it pulled me closer to my completion. It was no surprise that my body no longer wanted to participate in any way other than it was. Each time a part of me faltered I did not see it as new weakness but an invitation to step out of life and spend eternity in the limitless divinity that was God and All That Is.

I did not spend my last days idly at all though. I recited my last thoughts and philosophies that remain until this day. I prayed and sang hymns with my brothers when they came to visit.

This was how I left this life; singing a hymn one evening with Bernardo, one of my first devotees and Leo, another of my most beloved. We finished the song and I smiled upon them. That sense of completion that I knew would arrive was finally upon me.

Within that moment my eyesight cleared and behind Leo and Bernardo I saw the seraph who had come to me within the cave. All six of his wings were outstretched and he spoke.

"Are you ready?" he asked.

I nodded and smiled.

"What is it Francis?" asked Bernardo leaning in close.

"I have played my part. My act is complete. May Christ make you as complete as he has made me."

I said the words clearly and strong. Bernardo and Leo would say them many times over to all the brothers and anyone else they could.

They were my last words. I stepped from my body and the seraph took me by the hand.

"Your wounds are gone. You leave now free of all that your body carried for you," he said as the scene of my chamber dissolved beneath us.

Bernardo and Leo did not weep. Though they grieved in that moment they saw the blessing in the end of my physical suffering. They fell to their knees and prayed for my safe passage to heaven. They gave thanks to God for my presence in their lives and all our order.

Leo stood up and began to straighten my body. Then he pulled my sleeves to my elbows and the bed sheets to above my ankles. The sheet to my right was folded back so that the blood from my side could be seen.

"What are you doing?" Bernardo asked.

"Call all the brothers. Let them see how our Brother Francis lived and now he died as did Our Saviour."

Few had seen my stigmata. That had been my request. I had no desire for this gift to be paraded and looked upon like some novelty. In my heart I always believed that they were just for me. Now in my death that belief was set free and my legend was born.

Every brother of the monastery viewed my body and many touched the stigmata. They arrived in silence and left this way as well. Prayers were mouthed without sound and even once they left my presence they could not find any manner in which to discuss what they had seen.

My body was washed and anointed. It was placed within an open coffin in the Porziuncola for people to visit and pray over. The marks upon my wrists and feet were left uncovered so that anyone could see them and reflect upon my depth of connection to God with hope they would invite more of their own.

This included an envoy from the Vatican who not only came to pay his respects on their behalf but to witness and document what had been believed by many to be just rumours to exalt my death. When he stepped up to the coffin and looked upon my body he gasped and shook his head, then he looked up at the cross over the altar.

"You have shown us how true a servant he was," he cried out.

Within two years I was declared a saint; the quickest canonisation in history, bestowed upon me by Pope Gregory IX. The very next day he laid the first stone in what is now the grand basilica of Assisi. My body would be laid to rest within its lower basilica where it still is today.

Do not make pilgrimage to my body for your own saving or enlightenment. Come to visit my body in celebration of your own life. Come to Assisi because you too want to know the grandeur of God's love. Come to me and we will sing together.

Do not suffer for your enlightenment and awareness. Though I ended my days in physical pain I could still see the glory of being granted life. Each day we celebrate this essential truth we allow love and joy to conquer over hardship. Each day we delight in all of the Lord's creation we understand why he sent Christ to remind us of the glory he poured into each and every one of us.

Do not hesitate any longer my friends. Embrace this love and allow it into your life no matter where you are, or how you are living your life.

Love heals all because we are all born of the most magnificent love of our Creator. Return to that love and you too will become complete.

Amen.